MW00898694

WOK COOKBOOK FOR BEGINNERS

==

500+ Classic and Quick Recipes with Essential Ingredients for Wok Cooking

==

By

JEFFREY L. CADERON

TABLE OF CONTENTS

INTRODUCTION

Our family's eateries and our kitchens have traditionally relied heavily on woks. My folks sent me off to college with a wok and a cleaver. Before they left the house, I equipped each of my kids with their wok and cleaver. A permanent spot on our stove is reserved for my cast-iron Wok. My Wok is my go-to cooking tool, and I use it often. Deep-frying is only one of the numerous uses for it. Easy to use and great for cooking tasty stir-fries. Instead of having the oil splatter all over the place as it would in a shallow sauté pan or tiny pot, this one is deeper and has broader, sloping sides.

The wok is the best vessel to use when you want to reduce liquids and cook meat low and slow. Meat that is tender, juicy, and infused with the taste of the sauce results from poaching thinly sliced cattle, pig, or chicken after it has been stir-fried. Raise the heat and braise the heart for at least an hour if you want a heartier dish. Collagen in the heart will become more adaptable as a result. What does it signify? When you bite this meat on your tongue, it almost dissolves. Soups may also be prepared quite well in a wok. A stockpot with slanted sides is preferable to one with a flat bottom for heating liquids because it distributes the heat better. In addition, it is an efficient method for boiling noodles (mein), boiling vegetables, and cooking rice. Adding a rack behind the foot, above the water, and a dome-shaped cover on top transforms the piece into a steamer. Steaming is the ideal cooking method for just about everything. Steaming eliminates the need for oil while maintaining the food's flavor and texture. A wok may be converted into a smoker by using the rack and cover like a conventional smoker. To add flavor and aroma, the rice, tea, and spices are roasted in the bottom of the Wok. It's analogous to using wood chips for smoking or grilling outside. Smoking food in a wok is a breeze indoors or outdoors, with an exhaust fan and some open windows. It's incredible how versatile a wok can be.

The purpose of this book is to explain the capabilities of the task in great depth. You should read the first two chapters carefully before attempting any recipes. In this introductory chapter, learn about the origins of Chinese cuisine, the many types of woks, how to choose and maintain your wok, and some of the staples of a typical Chinese kitchen. The diverse applications of kitchen labor will be discussed in the next chapter. I discuss the knowledge and techniques that are crucial in each setting. The recipes in the subsequent chapters will be simple to master if you use what you learned in Chapters 1 and 2. You'll soon be able to work like a pro. You may customize the ingredients, method, and servings to create an infinite supply of unique recipes to share with friends and family. Get to woking, then!

CHAPTER ONE
GETTING STARTED

A wok would be the cooking utensil I'd take on a desert island if I had to choose just one. This is why: A wok is an excellent cooking tool since it can be used in place of both a pot and a frying pan. The borders of the cooking surface of this circular pan are rounded, so it heats up evenly and retains its heat for a more extended period. Its depth means that the contents won't sink to the bottom even when you give it a good stir. Professional cooks know that stir-fry is easiest to prepare and cook in a wok. However, this is but one method of cooking among many others. Deep frying, pan frying, broiling, poaching, steaming, roasting, braising, and smoking are some of the many cooking methods that may be accomplished in a wok. No matter what you're making, use a wok.

THE WOK AND CHINESE COOKING

Almost two millennia ago, the Han Dynasty in China produced the first known examples. You may think of a "wok" as a "pan." The importance of labor to people in Asia and beyond has grown throughout time. This kind of cookware is widely available in Asian countries. The Japanese word for "wok" is "chukanabe," which translates to "Chinese pan." The Indian phrase for labor is "cheena chatti," which translates to "Chinese pot." Kuali (meaning "little wok") and kawah (huge Wok) are the two main categories of employment in Malaysia. People of Chinese descent began arriving in the United States in the early nineteenth century in search of gold, constructing railways, finding work, supporting their families, and establishing the first Chinese restaurants. They took their creations along with them. The Wok's curving surface distributes heat uniformly throughout the contents. Most solid fuel stoves have circular bases that easily slide into the opening. High, curving sides are a trademark of most industrial constructions, which are often composed of cast iron or carbon steel. A 9- or 10-inch wok is suitable for cooking for one or two people, while a 12- or 14-inch wok is more suitable for cooking for two to six people. Larger than 16-inch works pose challenges when trying to cook them and need more room on the burner. A wok burner may fit on particular newer stoves. Significant 2- or 3-foot works may be purchased from restaurant supply companies, but most people only use them at home if they need professional burners and exhaust fans.

TYPES OF WOKS

Before making a final choice, consider the following woks and their advantages and disadvantages. If your Wok has a circular bottom, a steaming rack and ring are essential accessories.

Stainless Steel Wok

Because of its low maintenance requirements, stainless steel is often utilized for kitchen equipment. Stainless steel cookware is much simpler to maintain than nonstick or cast-iron options. Stainless steel has to be combined with copper or aluminum since it is a poor heat conductor. Food sticks and burns in low-quality stainless steel woks. Stainless steel can't be seasoned, but plenty of oil makes it less sticky. Stainless steel woks feature flat bases that are ideal for use on electric stovetops. Before you start cooking with an induction stove, be sure it reads "induction-ready."

Carbon Steel Wok

Most construction materials are made of carbon steel. It's simple and fast to create the non-stick patina. A carbon steel wok is ideal for stir-fry because to its durability, ease of use, and efficient heat transmission. Since carbon steel might rust if not correctly cared for, you should dry the Wok on the burner before storing it. Some people believe that coating metal with oil will prevent it from rusting. My carbon steel Wok is always hot and ready for use.

Cast-Iron Wok

Seasoning cast iron makes it nonstick and prevents food from sticking to it. There are works that have aged considerably. A 14-inch cast-iron wok weighs 12 pounds, making it much heavier than woks made from steel or stainless steel. Cast-iron woks take longer to heat up, but they're effective. Its thickness allows it to be both curved on the inside and flat on the bottom. A wok might crack if you put cold water in it and then placed it in boiling water. The acidity of tomato sauce or vinegar-based broths may help neutralize the heat.

Nonstick Wok

For stir-frying, considerable heat is required, which might damage nonstick woks. When a nonstick pan burns, it releases toxic fumes. They're great in stir-fries, braises, poaches, boils, and steams. Manufacturers recommend replacing nonstick cookware every two to three years, or as soon as it is damaged.

Electric Wok

The nonstick coatings on most electric woks are protected by a tiny heating element. Before heating the Wok, add the oil, and then cook the food in batches. Like nonstick pans, woks may be used for a variety of cooking methods, including sautéing, braising, poaching, and steaming. Pick one that has a 1500-watt element made of uncoated carbon or stainless steel.

CONFLICT BETWEEN ROUND AND FLAT-BOUND WOKS

Is it an induction, gas, or electric range? The kind of Wok you require is indicated by your stove. Historically, round-bottomed items were designed for use over gas, wood, or charcoal fires. The curved surface of the pan distributes heat more uniformly, creating hotter centers and cooler peripheries for cooking. Modern gas burners have spherical bases that rest on a ring for stability. Cooking using a round-bottomed pot or pan is difficult when using a flat surface. Flat-bottomed pans are required for use on electric burners. The thickness of the material allows for both the base and the inside to be balanced while yet being curved. To use a wok on an induction range, it must have a magnetic base or be specifically designed for use with induction cooking appliances.

WOK MAINTENANCE

Use your labor to make it live longer. Cast iron and carbon steel constructions are prime examples of this reality. Using your Wok for cooking reduces the likelihood of rusting. Patina improves the flavor of food cooked in a wok and makes it less likely to adhere to the pan. Cleaning with soapy water and a rough cloth will remove the seasoning.

Seasoning a Wok

Carbon steel and cast-iron woks must be used before they stop sticking. Here's what you need to do:
- Scrub your Wok with soap and water to eliminate the oil that keeps it from getting dirty. Dry.

- Put the wooden handles in the trash. If you can't, wrap the handles with paper towels. Aluminum foil should be used to cover the towels.
- Use avocado oil to clean the inside and outside of the Wok with a light touch.
- Put the lid on the Wok and bake it at 400°F for 15 minutes. Let the temperature go down.
- The third and fourth steps should be done three times. If you need to, re-wet the paper towels and place them on the wooden pieces. Then look at how they are doing.
- Before re-season your Wok, clean it with a rough pad and powder to eliminate all the rust. Rinse. Steps 3, 4, and 5 should be done again.

Cleaning a Wok

Here's how to clean your Wok:
- Use a non-scratch sponge and hot water to remove food that has become trapped.
- To dry the Wok, wipe it clean and heat it on medium for 5 minutes.
- Keep your work in a dry area if you will be using it for up to one week.
- A cloth or paper towel may line a nonstick wok while nesting other pans and pots.

Tips for maintaining your Wok's seasoning:
- After boiling, poaching, or steaming your work, ensure it is scorched and season it again.
- Acidic foods like tomatoes, vinegar, and citrus fruits should only take a short time to cook.
- The more you use a wok that doesn't stick, the better it will get.

TOOLS FOR COOKING IN A WOK

It would be best if you had a few things to cook with a wok. Start by getting cutting boards, a cleaver, a few bowls for prepping, and tools for moving hot ingredients around in the Wok. You can cook anything if you add a couple of racks and a cover for steaming or smoking.

Knives

Wok cooking depends on preparing bite-size ingredients. You should use a Chinese cleaver to do this job. It is easy to use because it has a large surface area, and you can use it to smash garlic and ginger. You can soften meat with the back of the blade and grind spices with the notch in the handle. It can also be used as a bench scraper to scoop up things.

Cutting Boards

Having two or three big cutting boards to prepare food is enough. Use one board for meat and fish and another for vegetables. Most people prefer wood and plastic.

Wok Spatula/Shovel/Spoon

I use a metal spoon with a long handle to stir things. Because the handle is so long, oil doesn't get on your hands. You can also mix sauces with it and serve them. The wok spatula and wok shovel both do a good job. A well-used wok can hold tools made of metal. Tools made of wood or silicone don't stick to things.

Steamer and Wok Cover

A simple steamer is a perforated rack that fits your work and holds food over boiling water. You also need a cover for the Wok. You can also buy stackable bamboo or metal steamers that fit in your work.

Prep Bowls

Get three or four bowls to organize and marinate the ingredients you've already made.

Cooking Chopsticks

Chopsticks are helpful kitchen tools. Most of the time, they are made of bamboo and are between 12 and 16 inches long. Chopsticks for cooking can be used to whisk and mix sauces and eggs, stir ingredients, and move noodles. They can also see how hot the oil is by putting the tips of the chopsticks in it. If bubbles come up, the oil is ready.

CHINESE KITCHEN STOCK UP

There are a lot of fresh and dried ingredients in the Chinese kitchen that are used to make the food taste the way it does. Each culture's food smells and tastes different because of a small number of things. This section will discuss common Asian ingredients that you might not find in a typical Western kitchen.

Fresh Ingredients

These are just a few fresh foods you can find in Asian markets. Some, like bok choy, napa cabbage, tofu, and ginger, are now easy to see in the produce section of many large grocery stores. I've added some more Asian vegetables you might not be familiar with.

BABY BOK CHOY

Baby bok choy is a different kind of bok choy than regular bok choy. It's half as big as the other one, tastes better, and can be picked earlier. Bok choy and baby bok choy have a lot of vitamins A and C.

BITTER MELON

Bitter melon is a long green squash that looks like a cucumber with bumps. You have to get used to the taste, which is the same as its name. It is also very healthy because it contains antioxidants, vitamins, and minerals.

CHINESE BROCCOLI

Chinese broccoli, also called gai lan, has crunchy green leaves on green stems. Like broccoli and bok choy, Gai Lan is in the cabbage family. It tastes more potent than both broccoli and bok choy.

BOK CHOY

Bok choy has smooth, white stalks, and its leaves are dark green. Shanghai bok choy has jade-green stalks. The stalks and leaves cook at different rates, so keep them separate and add them at other times.

DAIKON

Daikon is a mild Asian radish whose name means "big root." It looks like a white carrot, but some kinds are round, red, green, or watermelon-colored. You can eat the leaves, which taste spicy.

GARLIC

Garlic is used in the Chinese flavor base, which is very healthy food. Fresh cloves are the best. Peel the cloves and smash them with the flat side of the cleaver blade.

GINGER

Another part of the Chinese flavor base is fresh ginger root, which you can find in the produce section of most supermarkets. You don't have to peel it. Cut a 14-inch-wide cross-section, smash it with the flat side of a cleaver, and cut it into small pieces.

TOFU

Tofu is "vegan cheese." Soy milk is made into curds and whey by separating the curds from the whey. Firm tofu is pressed for a longer time than soft or silky tofu. Tofu contains nutrients and can be fermented differently to make different types.

MUSHROOMS

Asian mushrooms have a strong umami taste. Some grocery stores in the area sell shiitake and enoki mushrooms. You can often find king oysters or trumpet mushrooms in Asian markets.

NAPA CABBAGE

In the 1500s, Napa cabbage was grown for the first time near Beijing. It has stalks that grow in tight, oblong-shaped heads and leaves that are very soft and mild. Napa is also known as "Chinese cabbage."

ONIONS AND SCALLIONS

Yellow onions have a more robust flavor than red onions, which are more colorful. Scallions are a part of what gives Chinese food its taste. The white part tastes stronger on onion than the green shoots. Almost every dish needs both pieces to finish it off.

SEITAN

Seitan is made from wheat gluten and is a meat substitute. It contains a lot of protein. In Asian and health food stores, it is called "seitan." In regular stores that sell food, it is often labeled "vegetarian burger," "vegetarian chicken," or "meat substitute."

Pantry Ingredients

It would be best if you kept many of the following ingredients on hand because they are used in many recipes. With these, it will be easy to make a lot of tasty foods in a wok. Most of these ingredients are cheap, easy to find at the grocery store, and will last a long time in your pantry or fridge.

CORNSTARCH AND OTHER THICKENERS

Cornstarch is often used to thicken sauces and to "velvet" meat when cooking it in a wok to make it more tender. Other common thickeners are potato starch, tapioca, wheat flour, and rice flour.

OILS

Cooking oil shouldn't have a taste and shouldn't burn when heated to 350 F. Best is avocado oil. You can also use peanut, canola, and safflower oils. Don't let light get to oils. Oils like spicy sesame oil, garlic, ginger, basil, and truffle oil add flavor. You can't stir-fry with them because they can burn at lower temperatures. Don't let them see the light.

CHINESE RICE WINE

Food is seasoned, softened, and coated with Chinese cooking wine. You can find it online or in the international section or Asian market of a grocery store. Shaoxing cooking wine is a good choice. Shaoxing doesn't make wine? You can use pale, dry sherry or white wine instead of rice wine.

RICE VINEGAR

In China, black vinegar is made from toasted rice. Some vinegar has sugar, salt, and other flavors like herbs and fruits. Most western ciders and balsamic vinegar are more potent. If you want to use them in a recipe, I will mix them 50/50 with cooking wine.

VINEGAR AND WINE

Wine and vinegar were made more than 3,000 years ago. The complex tastes of wine come from the fermentation of fruits and grains. When wine is turned into vinegar, the umami taste gets more muscular, and there are more sweet and sour notes. As the food sits in the marinade, the vinegar and wine soften the meat because they are acidic and have water.

Sauces and Condiments

Spices and condiments are what give marinades and sauces their taste. Some herbs can be made from scratch, but good sauces that are already made are cheap, easy to use and keep well in the fridge.

DRIED CHILES

Chile is an American country. In the 15th century, explorers brought them to Europe and sent them to China along the Silk Road. Because of their heat, they became popular with Chinese cooks and are now used in many stir-fries.

DRIED MUSHROOMS

When dried mushrooms are added to recipes, they make them taste meaty and have a texture like meat. Most of the time, people eat black shiitake, tree ears, and cloud ears. Dried mushrooms have a much stronger umami flavor than fresh ones.

FERMENTED BLACK BEANS

Black soybeans fermented with salt, brine and sugar to make slightly chewy, umami-flavored dried beans are called fermented black beans. They're used to make food taste better. Also, they are often mashed up and put in sauces.

FISH SAUCE

This robust and fermented sauce adds a lot of umami flavor with just a few drops. Fish sauce smells terrible right out of the bottle, but once it's in a dish, the smell goes away. You don't have to keep the fish sauce in the fridge. Make sure it doesn't get on anything porous because it smells terrible!

HOISIN SAUCE

Hoisin is a sweet and salty glaze made of sweet potato, rice, sugar, soy sauce, vinegar, garlic, and chiles. Hoisin stays good in the fridge for a few months.

OYSTER SAUCE

A street vendor named Lee Kum Sheung left a pot of oyster stew on the back burner by accident in the 1800s. The next day, the noise had turned into a thick, dark, and savory liquid. Lee made a mistake, but he used it to start Lee Kum Kee, now one of the largest food companies in the world.

FIVE-SPICE POWDER

Some five-spice powders have more than five spices, but they all have cinnamon, cloves, fennel, Sichuan peppercorns, and star anise. People often use anise, cardamom, dried orange peel, ginger, and licorice.

PLUM SAUCE

This sweet-and-sour sauce is made by blending together plums, pineapple, peaches, and apricots. Sometimes a little bit of chile is added. It is often used as a dipping sauce and glaze on stir-fries or roasted meats.

SESAME SEEDS

People have been able to control sesame seeds for a long time. Since more than 5,000 years ago, they have been around. They taste like nuts and can be eaten raw, toasted, or blackened.

SICHUAN PEPPERCORNS

Sichuan peppercorns are not true peppercorns. They are the seed pods of the Chinese prickly ash. They taste like citrus and numb and tingle your tongue and mouth. They can be bought whole, ground, or in flavored oil.

SOY SAUCE

Soy sauce is made by giving soybeans, salt water, and wheat to a fungus called aspergillus to grow on. There are gluten-free, light, and dark varieties. Light soy is used in most recipes. It is thin and has a lot of salt. Light soy is different from low-sodium soy sauce, which tastes bland. Dark soy has been stored for longer and has sugars added to it. It thickens food and has less salt than light soy sauce. Soy sauce is thick when corn or potato starch is used to make a sweet glaze. Fermenting creamy soy sauce with rice makes gluten-free soy sauce. Soy sauce doesn't need to be stored in the refrigerator.

NUTS

Adding nuts or nut butter to recipes gives them to taste, texture, and more nutrients. People often use nuts like almonds, cashews, peanuts, and walnuts when cooking with a wok.

SPICES

Spices give food flavor, aroma, and heat. You can use them separately or all at once, like in five-spice powder. You can get better at cooking if you try these and other spices.

STAR ANISE

China has used this star-shaped seed pod with eight points for over 3,000 years. It is used in its whole form to give soups and braised dishes a sweet, licorice-like flavor. It is also in five-spice powder.

Canned Goods

Even though these recipes focus on fresh produce, some ingredients can only be found locally in cans because of distance, weather, or time of year.

BAMBOO SHOOTS

They are crunchy and taste nutty. It would help if you boiled fresh bamboo shoots. Bamboo shoots in a can have already been cooked, and you can heat them up in minutes.

BEAN SPROUTS

Bean sprouts are full of healthy things. Even though canned bean sprouts aren't as crunchy or tasty as fresh ones, they may be safer to eat. The same conditions that help fresh sprouts grow also help bacteria grow. If you cook with raw sprouts, you can kill germs by putting them in soups or stir-fries for a minute or two.

STRAW MUSHROOMS

Rice straw is used to grow straw mushrooms. They taste weak and are a good meat substitute. Before you use canned mushrooms, drain and rinse them.

WATER CHESTNUTS

Water chestnuts are a sweet root vegetable that has a nice crunch. You might be able to buy them fresh at an Asian market near you, but you can get them in a can at most stores.

Noodles and Rice

Many of the dishes in this book go well with rice or noodles. Rice is the most common grain in Asia. It is grown in more than 40,000 different types all over the world. The most common types of rice are Indica long-grain rice and Japonica short-grain rice. Rice with long grains has less starch than rice with short grains. In China, rice, wheat, buckwheat, potato starch, and beans make many different noodles. They are cooked in different ways and come in different shapes and thicknesses. Here are the three kinds that are used most often in a stir-fry.

WHITE RICE

Most Chinese food is made with long-grain white rice. The jasmine rice from Thailand and the basmati rice from the foothills of the Himalayas are two other types of rice. Japonica rice is Japanese rice with medium-sized grains that is stickier and easier to eat with chopsticks.

YAO MEIN

Asian stores sell these tiny egg noodles, both fresh and frozen. They are often already cooked.

CHOW MEIN

Fried noodles are what chow mein means. Think of chow mein as stir-fry on top of crispy fried noodles.

LO MEIN

In Cantonese, the word for "stirred noodles" is "lo mein." During the stir-frying process, cooked noodles are mixed in with the other ingredients. This makes the noodles softer and more tender.

CHAPTER TWO
TECHNIQUES FOR WOK

I'm sure you can't wait to use your Wok for cooking. But before you heat your Wok, it's essential to have everything ready and a plan for how you'll make a dish from start to finish. It's great to be able to improvise, but you need to know and be good at a lot of things before you can spice things up. In this chapter, I'll show you how to use your Wok for cooking and what steps to take. Knowing about and using these routines and practices will save time, energy, and ingredients. As Xun Kuang concluded above, "Involve me, and I learn."

PROPER PREP

Read the recipe twice. This will give you time to get the right tools, double-check the ingredients, and get used to the cooking process.

Use room-temperature ingredients. For thousands of years, cooks didn't have any way to keep food cold. In the original recipes, you had to use fresh ingredients. As the food in the Wok cools, the Wok will also cool, changing how the food is cooked.

Before heating your Wok, prepare all of your ingredients. For example, you have to time stir-frying down to the minute. Once cooking has started, it can't be stopped. You might need more time to find and prepare missing materials, so ensure everything is ready before you start.

Cut ingredients into "chopstick-size" pieces. Bite-sized pieces of different sizes. Cook quickly and evenly, especially when making a stir-fry. When parts are cut into slices, there are more places to marinate, sear, and seal fluids. Most wok recipes don't call for details of the finished meal to be cut up.

Arrange ingredients in cooking order. If you set up the elements ahead of time, you'll be ready to put them in the Wok. By putting the ingredients in bowls in the order they'll go into the Wok, you can practice the recipe in your head. Your guests will be amazed by how well-organized and comfortable you are in the kitchen and how tasty the food is.

Serve and eat ASAP! The best time to eat something is right after it's done cooking. Only the cook can check to see if the food is done when the work is taken off the heat. The next best thing is to have a hot rice dish or noodles ready to be served.

THE IMPORTANCE OF MISE EN PLACE

The French phrase "mise en place" means "to set up." It is pronounced, "MEEZ-an-plaz." All the ingredients have been cut, marinated, smoothed, measured, put in the right place, and ready to go. "Mise en place" means "I am ready, focused, centered, and in the right place" when stir-frying. Here are a few essential things to do to get ready.

- Thinly slicing animal proteins like chicken and beef helps them cook quickly. Before slicing the meat, putting it in the freezer for 30 minutes makes it easier to cut. Make sure the roots are cool to the touch before you start cooking.
- If the recipe calls for it, you can "velvet" your proteins by marinating them in cornstarch, soy sauce, wine, spices, and flavored oil.
- The rest of the ingredients need to be cut up, so they are easy to eat.
- Measure and mix all of the sauce's ingredients. Set aside until you're ready to go.

- Place everything where it belongs.
- Ensure the bowls and utensils are warm, and the rice or noodles are ready to eat. Make sure that the drinks are prepared as well.
- Now, heat your Wok, get your tools, add some oil, and start at the beginning of the line of well-organized ingredients.

STIR-FRYING

Stir-fry was the first meal that was made in just one pot. In a wok, you quickly toss soft, juicy ingredients about the size of chopsticks with fragrant ingredients like ginger and garlic in oil that is so hot that it smokes. Add a tasty sauce and a fresh topping before you turn off the heat. Stir-frying is a fast way to cook that uses time, energy, and resources well. Also, it's easy to clean. Rinse the Wok with hot water, dry it, and put it away (or, if you're like me, leave it on the stove, so it's ready for your next meal!). Here are some tips on how to stir-fry well. First, put everything where it belongs.

Velveting and Marinating

You can make proteins more tender, juicy, and flavorful by soaking them in liquids or covering them with dry spices (called a "dry rub"). Cornstarch, rice wine, oil, and sometimes an egg are mixed together to make a glaze that seals the meat as it cooks in the Wok. This keeps the heart juicy, tender, and full of flavor. Even though marinating and velveting have different goals, but I've found that they can be done in one step using the same ingredients. This makes the process easier and gets excellent results at the same time.

Heating the Wok for stir-fry

When you stir-fry, you sear the food at a high temperature, so the work needs to be at the right temperature before you add the food. Turn on your exhaust fan and open some nearby windows when you stir-fry. Some people put a shower cap on their kitchen smoke alarm to turn it off for a short time. It is hot enough to stir-frying in when the work starts to smoke. At this point, you should add the oil. Remember the saying, "Hot wok, cold oil." You can coat the bottom of the Wok by tilting and swirling it, or you can use your wok tool to move the oil around the Wok if you are cooking something heavier. If your work doesn't stick, put oil in it before you heat it. When the oil shimmers or moves, it is ready to use for stir-frying.

Adding the Ingredients

Once your Wok and oil are hot enough, add your ingredients to the recipe's order. Things that take longer to cook should be stir-fried first to keep cooking while other items are added. If you have carrots, onions, and shrimp, start with the carrots. The shrimp and onions come next. The carrots will also be ready when the onions and shrimp are done.

Tossing vs. Stirring

As the name of the method suggests, the stir-fry ingredients must always be moving. It doesn't matter if you stir and flip them by lifting and tilting your carbon steel wok or if you stir and scan them with your spatula in your black cast-iron Wok. Most of the oil and juices will flow toward the center of the Wok, where it is the hottest. As you toss or stir, move the ingredients from the center to the more excellent edges and the food from the edges to the center to sear in the hot oil and let their juices flavor the other ingredients. A wok with a single long handle is best for tossing ingredients. If it's bigger than 12 inches, the long handle should be paired with a shorter one. The motion of throwing stars with the tip of the handle facing away from you and up. As the work tilts forward, the food will move away from you. As you pull the Wok back toward you, tilt the handle down. This makes the food move up the curve of the Wok, back toward you, and over the middle of the Wok. It takes some time to get used to, but it's fun!

Thickening, Saucing and Garnishing

Before turning off the heat and serving the stir-fry, the last thing to do is add the sauce to give it flavor. Stir-frying is a "dry process" in which ingredients are seared in hot oil. Most people mess up when making stir-fry by adding sauce too early. If too many wet ingredients are put into the Wok, or a liquid sauce is added, the Wok will cool down, and the stir-frying process will stop. The food will stick together and become wet. So, put sauce liquids in at the end. Mix the sauce ahead of time, so it's ready to go when the stir-fry is done. If you want a thicker glaze, you can add cornstarch or something else to the sauce to make it more comprehensive. You can also sprinkle the cornstarch into the stir-fry as you mix the ingredients and seasoning. The cornstarch will dissolve and quickly turn into a glaze when you stir or toss the food. Chop up garnishes like scallions and squeeze them in your hands as you sprinkle them over the finished stir-fry. Serve right away.

WOK-HEI

Wok Hei, also known as "breath of the wok," is a smoky flavor from vaporizing and burning oil while stir-frying. This is best done in restaurants with carbon works, powerful burners, and industrial exhaust fans. Due to power and ventilation issues, it is hard to get wok hei on a gas stove at home or to get something close to it on an electric stove. Chao, the oldest method, means "to fry." Heat the oil until it starts to smoke, then move on. Avocado oil is the best because it doesn't smoke until it reaches over 500 F. Canola, safflower, and peanut oils work almost as well. Use avocado oil and a flat-bottomed wok on an electric stove to make something similar to wok hei. The words bao or pow mean "to pop" in another style. Bring the Wok to a red glow over a flame. Flames and smoke are made when oil and ingredients are thrown in quickly. Bao stir-frying is fast and exciting, just like its name. It should be done in kitchens with enough space and ventilation or outside on fire (with a fire extinguisher handy!) If you try to stir-fry bao with the recipes in this book, expect it to take half as long per ingredient and take twice as much work as Chao.

BRAISING

The Western way of cooking meat for hours at a time, which breaks down the connective tissues, is different from braising in a wok (as in stews). There are two steps to cooking in a wok most of the time. Proteins quickly stir-fried with aromatics and hearty vegetables to make new flavor combinations. After you stir-fry the ingredients, barely cover them with a rich sauce and turn the heat down to a low simmer. The well-known recipe for Ma Po Tofu uses this method of braising. In hong shao, which means "red cooked" in Chinese, meat is braised in sweet, dark soy sauce. This is a well-known way to cook. Red Cooked Pork (Hong Shao Rou) is an example. This used to be one of Chairman Mao's favorite dishes.

STEAMING

Since you can steam in a wok, you can see how useful they are. Putting food on a rack above boiling water and covering it with a dome-shaped lid can be used to cook vegetables, meats, dumplings, bread, and even desserts. Steam cooks food faster than boiling water because it is hotter. Smoke is much less dense than boiling water and cooks with moist, gentle heat. Also, steamed food keeps its flavor, minerals, and nutrients, which would be lost if boiled or poached. Burning is also a great way to cook delicate foods like fish and seafood with mild flavors, such as shrimp and shellfish. The steam gets everywhere, so you don't have to stir or flip the food. Vegetables keep their shapes, flavors, and colors better when gently steamed. When meat is cooked, it stays juicy and tender. Put a rack with holes in your work so that it is about an inch above the water that is just simmering. This will cause the water to start boiling. If the holes are small enough, food can go right on the frame. If you use a cake rack to hold the food, put a plate on top. You can also use traditional bamboo steamers with dome-shaped lids. Different sizes are available.

Because the sides of the Wok are curved, any size steamer will fit as long as it is smaller than the Wok's diameter. This steamer is suitable for feeding a large group because the pots can be stacked on each other. Because the steam rises, everything gets cooked evenly. Watch the water level, though. If it evaporates, it could spark a fire in the steamer. There's no need to take the steamers out when the water level gets low. To fill it up, pour a cup of water between the edge of the Wok and the steamer's side.

SMOKING

Smoking food is one of the oldest ways to add flavor and keep it fresh. It is still used a lot in many dishes around the world. Archaeological records show that people who lived in caves around 400,000 years ago may have accidentally preserved meat by hanging it near the fires they used for heat and light. "Hot-smoking" is a method for cooking food that uses higher temperatures than "cold-smoking," which keeps food fresh. To smoke food, you put a rack in your Wok, put the food you want to smoke on the frame, and cover it tightly. When you smoke, instead of simmering water to make steam, you burn a mixture of sugar, tea leaves, wood chips, and spices in an open or perforated foil packet. This makes the food taste and smells like smoke. You can smoke inside with the windows and the exhaust fan on high (not a recirculating filter). You should also cover your smoke alarm or turn it off for now. But if you can, I recommend smoking food outside because even if the lid fits well, smoke will often escape from the Wok. You can try smoking different things together, like tea leaves, wood chips, rice, cornmeal, citrus peels, brown sugar, cinnamon, and other spices. Smoking can also be the first step in "twice-cooked" recipes, in which the food is smoked and then steamed or braised. A wok can be used to cook fish quickly and then lightly smoke it. Put a little water in the hot Wok without removing the lid. Be careful, though, because adding water to the heat will quickly make a big head of scalding steam.

FRYING

Most people use the wok to stir-fry, but it can also be used to deep-fry, shallow-fry, or pan-fry. The main difference between how much oil is used for cooking each of the three. One thing they all need before they start frying is for the oil to be hot. When you deep-fry, you use the most fat. Items should be able to float in the oil, so it should be deep enough.

The oil is ready when you dip the end of a wooden chopstick into it, and bubbles form around it. You can also use a thermometer and start deep-frying when the temperature reaches 350 F. If the heat isn't high enough, the food won't brown and get crisp. If the temperature goes above 400 F, the food will burn on the outside before the inside is ready. In shallow frying, only half of what is cooking on the bottom of the wok is covered by oil. This method is used when the breading on the food is dry, and you want it to stay on the food as it is fried. The breading will stick to the food when it hits the bottom of the wok.

When the browning is done on one side, you flip it over to brown the other side. Pan-frying, similar to stir-frying, uses the least amount of oil. The only difference is that you put the food in the pan and let it brown on one side for a few minutes before turning it over to brown the other. When you fry food in a pan, you don't stir it.

DIM SUM, SOUPS, AND SAUCES

DEEP-FRIED SALMON AND MISO WONTONS

Wontons are a type of Chinese dumpling that have a thin layer of dough on the outside and a tasty filling on the inside. Umami and seafood flavors burst out of these crunchy little bags of taste.

INGREDIENTS:

- 1 (8-ounce) skinless salmon fillet
- 1 tablespoon white or yellow miso
- 2 fresh garlic cloves, crushed and chopped
- 1 teaspoon toasted sesame oil
- 1 tablespoon soy sauce
- 1 (12-ounce) package square wonton wrappers
- 2 cups oil for deep-frying

INSTRUCTIONS:

1. Mix the salmon, miso, garlic, olive oil, and soy sauce in a food processor.
2. If you put a wonton wrapper on a table so it looks like a baseball field, you are sitting behind home plate.
3. Fill some water into a small bowl. Paint the water along the lines with a clean fingertip.
4. Put a teaspoon of the filling in the middle, where the pitcher's mound would be.
5. Bring a home plate to second base and fold the wrapper into a triangle to keep the food inside. Fill in what's missing.

6. Heat the oil in the wok until it bubbles when a wooden chopstick is dropped into it or until it hits 350°F.
7. Fry the wontons in oil on both sides until they are golden brown. You can use any sauce you like.

LION'S HEAD MEATBALLS (SHI ZI TOU)

big meatballs or eight smaller ones called "cubs." Originally, shi zi, also known as "lion's head" meatballs, were about the size of tennis balls and were served on Chinese cabbage leaves (the "mane"). The pork, garlic, ginger, and scallions give the food a simple, classic flavor. Maybe these are just young cats!

INGREDIENTS:
- 1 pound ground pork
- 1 tablespoon chopped fresh ginger
- 4 garlic cloves, crushed and chopped
- 4 scallions, both white and green parts, minced
- 2 tablespoons dark soy sauce
- 2 tablespoons Shaoxing cooking wine
- 1 large egg
- ¼ cup cornstarch
- 1 teaspoon spicy sesame oil
- 2 cups cooking oil
- 2 cups broth (chicken, beef, or vegetable)
- 2 cups coarsely chopped
- Chinese cabbage (bok choy or napa)

INSTRUCTIONS:

1. In a big bowl, mix together the pork, ginger, garlic, scallions, soy sauce, wine, egg, cornstarch, sesame oil, and cornstarch.
2. You can make 4 big meatballs or 8 small ones, depending on what you want.
3. Heat the oil in the wok until it bubbles when a wooden chopstick is dropped into it or until it hits 350°F. Fry the meatballs in the same way until they are all brown. Put away and bring out. Pour out the fat.
4. Simmer the stock in the wok over medium heat for 10 minutes.
5. Add the cabbage leaves and let them cook for about 5 minutes, or until they are soft.
6. Put the meatballs on top of cooked cabbage leaves.

STEAMED SCALLION BUNS (HUA JUAN) VEGETARIAN

The dough for these buns is the same as that for steamed baos, but we twist these to make them look more interesting. If you want to impress someone or celebrate a special event, you can make these. The hardest part of the process is waiting for the dough to rise. The buns look like they would be hard to make, but they aren't.

INGREDIENTS:
- ¾ cup whole milk, at room temperature
- 1 tablespoon sugar
- 1 teaspoon active dry yeast
- 2 cups all-purpose flour
- 1 teaspoon baking powder

- ¾ teaspoon kosher salt, divided
- 2 tablespoons sesame oil, divided
- 2 teaspoons Chinese five-spice powder, divided
- 6 scallions, both white and green parts, thinly sliced

INSTRUCTIONS:

1. In a liquid measuring cup, mix the milk, sugar, and yeast together. Give it 5 minutes to sit so the yeast can do its job.

2. Mix the flour, baking powder, and 14 teaspoons of salt in a large bowl or with the dough hook tool on a stand mixer set to low. Pour the milk mixture into the bowl and stir it for 30 seconds. Mix for 5 minutes on high speed, or 6 to 8 minutes by hand, until the dough is soft and stretchy. Put the dough on a flat surface and knead it by hand a few times until it is smooth. Put the dough in a bowl, cover it with a towel, and let it sit for 10 minutes.

3. Put two pieces of dough together. Roll one piece into a 15-by-18-inch square with a rolling pin. Paint the dough with 1 tablespoon of sesame oil. Use 1 teaspoon of five-spice powder and 1/4 teaspoon of salt to season the food. Add half of the onions and use your fingers to work them into the dough.

4. Roll up the dough like a cinnamon roll, starting from the long side. Cut the rolled log into eight pieces that are all the same size. To make a bun form, stack two pieces so that the cut sides are visible.

5. Use a chopstick to press down on the stack along its length. Some of the fillings will come out as a result. Put away that chopstick. Pull the two ends of the dough apart a little bit with your fingers to stretch it. Then, curl the ends under and pinch them together.

6. Put the bun on a 3x3-inch square piece of parchment paper and put it in a steamer basket to rise. Repeat with the rest of the dough, making sure to leave at least 2 inches between each bun. If you need more room, you can use a second steamer basket. There should be 8 buns with twists. Cover the jars with plastic wrap and leave them for an hour or until they are twice as big.

7. About two inches of water should be in the wok, and the steamer pan should be inside the wok. The water level should be 14 and 1/2 inches above the bottom of the steamer, but not so high that it hits the bottom of the basket. Over medium-high heat, bring the water to a boil. Put the lids on the steamer baskets.

8. Set the heat to medium and let the pot cook for 15 minutes. If you need to, add more water to the wok. Take the baskets off the heat and keep them covered for 5 more minutes. Place the buns on a serving dish.

SMALL DUMPLINGS (YAU GOK)

The form of these sweet little dumplings is like old Chinese silver ingots. At the Lunar New Year, people eat them because they think it will bring them luck and money. I like them any time of the year.

INGREDIENTS:

- 1 cup sweetened coconut flakes
- 1 cup chopped honey-glazed peanuts
- ⅓ cup toasted sesame seeds
- 3 tablespoons brown sugar
- 1 (12-ounce) package of round wonton wrappers Oil for deep-frying

INSTRUCTIONS:

1. In a small bowl, mix together the brown sugar, coconut, peanuts, sesame seeds, and sesame seeds.
2. Fill the middle of a shell with a teaspoon of filling.
3. Pour water into a small bowl. Wet the edge of the wrapper with a clean fingertip, and then fold it in half to cover the center. To seal, press.
4. Use your fingers to moisten the curved and covered edge of the dumpling.
5. Fold the left side of the dumpling over 1/8 inch and press it down with your thumb to make a small crease. It would help if you were looking at the bent edge.
6. For the second pleat, move 1/8 inch to the right of the first one and grab the folded edge of the dough with your thumb and fingers. Fold the edge over by 1/8 inch and press hard with your thumb on the fold. This is the most important step. When you crimp the sides, you'll get

bumps if you don't press down on each fold and leave that 1/8 inch of fold alone.

7. Repeat step 6 at regular intervals and push down hard on the dumpling to close it. It would help if you ended up with a small dumpling that looks like a crescent and a seal that looks like a bent rope. Use the same method for the rest of the wraps and filling.

8. Oil in the pot should be heated to 350 F. Fry the dumplings for 10 to 20 seconds in hot oil, or until they are golden brown.

9. The food should be drained and put on a paper towel.

SWEET DUMPLINGS (TANG YUAN)

Tang Yuan, a sweet treat made with rice flour, is served at the Lunar New Year. It means "first evening" in English. Since dumplings are round, they are also served at weddings and family parties because they represent coming together.

INGREDIENTS:

- ¼ cup toasted sesame seeds (toasted, black, or mixed)
- 2 tablespoons granulated sugar
- ¼ cup smooth or crunchy peanut butter
- 1 cup glutinous rice flour, plus
- ¼ cup for kneading
- ½ cup hot tap water

INSTRUCTIONS:

1. Use a food mixer to mix the sesame seeds and sugar, but don't make a paste. You can use a mixer, a food processor, or a mortar and pestle to do this.

2. Mix the sugar and seeds into the peanut butter, and then put the mixture in the refrigerator.
3. In another bowl or food processor, mix the sticky flour and hot tap water, and knead for 10 to 15 minutes by hand or 2 or 3 minutes in the food processor, until a smooth dough forms.
4. Bring a lot of water to a boil in a big pot.
5. Divide the dough into equal pieces and roll each one into a ball about 1 inch in diameter.
6. You should cut the center in half and roll each half into a 1.5-inch ball.
7. Flatten a ball of dough a bit and wrap it around a ball of filling.
8. Boil the dumplings for 15 minutes, or until they float to the top. Serve with some of the water used to cook it.

POTSTICKERS (JIAOZI)

People say that a cook for a ruler saved his own life by pouring water on some dumplings that were on fire. The emperor's favorite meal was cooked dumplings with a crispy bottom. The dumplings should be served with a bowl of soy sauce to dip them in. If you like things hot, you can add a little chili oil to the soy sauce.

INGREDIENTS:

- 8 ounces ground pork
- 4 scallions, both white and green parts, minced
- ½ cup chopped mushrooms
- 2 garlic cloves, crushed and chopped
- 1 tablespoon chopped fresh ginger
- 1 tablespoon hoisin sauce

- 1 tablespoon soy sauce
- 1 (12-ounce) package round wonton wrappers
- 2 tablespoons cooking oil
- ¼ cup water

INSTRUCTIONS:

1. In a medium bowl, mix together the pork, onions, mushrooms, garlic, ginger, hoisin sauce, and soy sauce.
2. Fill the middle of each shell with 1 tablespoon of filling. Keep everything inside the first 14 inches.
3. Pour water into a small bowl. Put water around the edge of the package with a clean fingertip.
4. At 11, 12, and 1 o'clock, fold the edge of the wrapper three times.
5. Fold the paper in half, move the point from 6 to 12, and then seal the dumpling.
6. Press down on the bottom of the dumpling to make it flat. Do the same thing with the rest of the dumplings and covers.
7. Mix the oil around the bottom of the pot and heat it on high until it shimmers.
8. Put the dumplings in the pan and fry them for two or three minutes, or until the bottoms are golden brown.
9. Pour the water into the side of the pan and use the lid to cover most of it. Cover the rest of the way, and steam for about 2 minutes, or until all the water has drained. Be careful, because mist could form right away.
10. Carefully take the wok off of the heat and serve the dumplings with a sauce to dip them in.

CHICKEN HOT POT (GAI BO)

This is a chicken stew that looks and tastes good. It has Chinese spices and soy sauce in it. Using chicken legs without the skin and bones makes the process easier, but you can also use chicken with bones to add more flavor to the broth.

INGREDIENTS:

- 1 pound boneless, skinless chicken thighs, cut into to 2-inch pieces
- 2 tablespoons cooking oil
- 2 (1-inch) pieces of fresh ginger, sliced diagonally
- 4 (1-inch) pieces of cassia bark or cinnamon bark
- 3 black cardamom pods or
- 2 white pods and
- 1 black pod 2 whole star anise pods
- 1 tablespoon dark soy sauce
- 2 teaspoons sea salt
- 1½ teaspoons Shaoxing cooking wine or dry sherry
- 2 cups water 3 to
- 7 spicy green chiles, sliced diagonally

INSTRUCTIONS:

1. Put the chicken in a pot with hot water for 5 minutes to cook it. Use a bowl to rinse and drain to get rid of any food.
2. Put the oil in the wok and heat it on high until it starts to shimmer. Stir-fry the chicken and ginger for about 5 minutes, or until the chicken is browned.
3. Next, add the cardamom, star anise, and cassia bark. Stir-fry for another minute or two, or until the food starts to smell good.

4. Stir-fry for one more minute to mix in the wine, salt, and dark soy sauce.
5. Put the water in, and slowly heat it. You can make the food spicy by adding as many or as few peppers as you want. Let it cook on low heat for 20 to 25 minutes, until the flavors come together. Prepare hot.

SHRIMP DUMPLINGS (HAR GAO)

After shumai, shrimp dumplings, or har ago, are one of the most famous types of dim sum. Imagine shrimp with different tastes and crunchy water chestnuts wrapped in soft, delicate dumpling dough. Because the dough contains wheat starch, the cakes almost look clear. Getting the wrapper right may take some practice, but it is well worth the time.

INGREDIENTS:

For the filling
- 1 pound peeled and deveined shrimp, coarsely chopped
- ¼ cup diced water chestnuts
- 2 tablespoons cornstarch
- 1½ tablespoons sesame oil
- 2 teaspoons soy sauce
- 2 tablespoons finely chopped fresh cilantro (optional)

For the wrappers
- 1¼ cups wheat starch
- 2 tablespoons tapioca flour
- 1¼ cup boiling water
- 1 teaspoon cooking oil

For the filling,

INSTRUCTIONS:

1. In a big bowl (if you're using one), mix the shrimp, water chestnuts, cornstarch, sesame oil, soy sauce, and cilantro. Blend well.
2. Put the mixture in the refrigerator for at least 30 minutes to combine the tastes. To make the boxes and bags.
3. In a big bowl, mix the tapioca flour and wheat starch.
4. As you stir, slowly pour the hot water into the flour mixture. Keep doing this until the dough starts to come together into a ball.
5. Cover the bowl with a wet towel and let the dough cool before working with it.
6. A small rolling pin, a cutting board, and a little cooking oil on your hands will keep the dough from sticking.
7. Spend two or three minutes kneading it.
8. Take about a teaspoon of dough and gently roll it into a ball.
9. Make a small pancake about 3 inches across with the dough. How to Cook Dumplings
10. Set up a bamboo steamer in a wok. You can cover the inside of the steamer with parchment paper or napa cabbage leaves.
11. Fill the middle of a wrapper with about 1 teaspoon of the shrimp filling.
12. Make 7 to 10 pleats on one side of the wrapper, then fold the other side toward the pleated side to close the dumpling.
13. Place the dumplings in the bamboo cooker. Repeat with the rest of the filling and wraps.
14. About an inch of water should be in the wok, and the steamer baskets should be in the wok. Bring the water to a boil over medium-high heat. Cover the steamer baskets with their lids.

15. Turn the heat to medium and let the meat steam for 5 minutes or until it is done. Move to a plate to serve.

SOUP DUMPLINGS (XIAOLONGBAO)

One of the most famous dishes from the Chinese region of Sichuan, where Shanghai is located, are these small dumplings filled with soup. Xiaolongbao is also called Shanghai soup dumplings because Shanghai is the biggest city in Sichuan and one of China's three most populated places.

INGREDIENTS:

- 1 cup hot tap water
- 1 teaspoon chicken, beef, or pork bouillon
- 1 (¼-ounce) package of unflavored gelatin
- 4 ounces ground pork
- 2 scallions, both white and green parts, minced
- 1 teaspoon chopped fresh ginger
- 1 garlic clove, crushed and chopped
- 1 teaspoon soy sauce
- 1 teaspoon sugar
- 1 teaspoon toasted sesame oil
- 20 (4-inch) round dumpling wrappers (If you use more miniature wrappers, they will be harder to fold)
- 4 to 6 lettuce leaves

INSTRUCTIONS:

1. Mix the hot tap water, the bouillon, and the gelatin in a medium bowl until the gelatin is dissolved. Put it in the fridge or freezer until it turns into jelly.
2. Combine the pork, scallions, ginger, garlic, soy sauce, sugar, and sesame oil in a big bowl.

3. Mix well after adding the gelatinized water to the meat mixture.
4. About 1 tablespoon of filling should go in the middle of the paper. Make sure there is no filling on the side of the paper that measures 14 inches.
5. To make a dumpling, hold the wrapper in your less dominant hand and make creases with your more dominant hand, turning the wrapper as you go and bringing the dough together to look like a "moneybag." When you get to the end, turn the top to close the package.
6. Put the lettuce leaves in the steamer basket and the dumplings on top of the lettuce. Repeat with the rest of the filling and the wraps.
7. About two inches of water should be in the wok, and the steamer pan should be inside the wok. The water level should be 14 and 1/2 inches above the bottom of the steamer but not so high that it hits the bottom of the basket. Bring the water to a boil over medium-high heat, then put the lid on the steamer basket and cover it with the lid.
8. Turn the heat down to medium and steam the food for 10 minutes or until it's done.
9. Put the food on a chopstick and eat it right away. Be careful! There will be hot soup inside the dumplings.

QUICK STEAMED PORK BUNS (CHAR SIU BAO)

In dim sum places, "barbecue pork buns," or "charsiu bao," are served on rolling steam carts. Bits of sweet and salty roasted pork belly are mixed into the soft, hot dough. My mom speeds up this dish by using buttermilk biscuit dough from the store that has already been chilled.

INGREDIENTS:

- 1 tablespoon cooking oil
- 1 pound pork belly or pork shoulder, diced into ¼-inch pieces
- ½ cup char siu sauce (such as Lee Kum Kee or Ah-So)
- 2 tablespoons brown sugar
- 1 (16-ounce) can of buttermilk biscuits (8 large)

INSTRUCTIONS:

1. Put the oil in the wok and heat it high until it shatters. Stir-fry the pork for 2 minutes.
2. Turn the stove down to medium. Add the char siu sauce and brown sugar, and cook for 5 minutes or until the pork is done. Put it somewhere to cool down.
3. Use the dough to make four rounds.
4. Put two tablespoons of pork (called "charsiu") in the middle of each dough circle (called "bao").
5. To make a bun, pull the edges of the circle toward the middle, pinch and twist the dough together, and cover the filling fully.
6. Put parchment paper on the steamer tray, and leave at least 1 inch between each bao. They'll keep getting bigger.

7. About two inches of water should be in the wok, and the steamer pan should be inside the wok. The water level should be 14 and 1/2 inches above the bottom of the steamer but not so high that it hits the bottom of the basket. Bring the water to a boil over medium-high heat, then put the lid on the steamer basket and cover it with the lid.

8. Turn the heat down to medium and steam the food for 10 minutes or until it's done. Serve right away.

SUI MAI DUMPLINGS

Sui Mai, which means "to cook and sell," was made during the Qing era in the 1600s. Chinese chefs took this famous dim sum dish to Japan, Korea, and Southeast Asia. Three dried shiitake mushrooms that have been washed and chopped. If you want to use whole mushrooms, cut off the tough stems.

INGREDIENTS:
- 8 ounces ground pork
- 1 tablespoon sugar
- 1 tablespoon Shaoxing cooking wine
- 1 teaspoon soy sauce
- 4 ounces shrimp, peeled and deveined
- 1 (12-ounce) package of round wonton wrappers

INSTRUCTIONS:
1. Pulse the pork, mushrooms, sugar, wine, and soy sauce in a food processor.
2. Add the shrimp and roughly chop them until they are all over the dish.

3. Make an "O" with your thumb and fingers to put together dumplings. Place a wrapper over the O and gently push a teaspoon of filling and the wrapper down into the O.
4. With a butter knife, gently press and spread on more filling until the top edge of the wrapper is covered.
5. Press down on the bottom of the dumpling to flatten it, and then use your fingers to roll it up.
6. Place the dumplings on parchment paper and put them in a steamer. Repeat with the rest of the filling and wraps.
7. About 2 inches of water should be in the wok, and the steamer should go there. The water level should be 14 and 1/2 inches above the bottom of the steamer but not so high that it hits the bottom of the basket. Put the steamer's lid on and bring the water to a boil over medium-high heat.
8. Turn the heat down to medium and steam the food for 10 minutes or until it's done. Serve right away.

EGG DROP SOUP (DAN HUA TANG)

Dan Hua Tang, which means "egg flower soup," is another name for egg drop soup. In the broth, the thin threads of poached eggs look like flowers opening up. People think it's very healthy because it has a lot of protein and not much fat or carbs.

INGREDIENTS:

- 8½ cups vegetable broth, divided
- 1 ounce dried, sliced shiitake or tree ear mushrooms
- ¼ cup cornstarch
- 4 large eggs, beaten
- 4 scallions, both white and green parts, cut into ¼-inch pieces

INSTRUCTIONS:

1. Mix the mushrooms and 8 cups of stock in the wok. Get it to boil.
2. Mix the last 1/2 cup of broth with 1/4 cup of cornstarch to make a slurry in a small bowl.
3. Stir the cornstarch slurry into the boiling stock until the broth thickens and becomes clear. You can change the soup is thickness or thickness by adding more or less of the slurry.
4. As you slowly pour the eggs into the wok, stir the broth in one way. About a minute should be enough time to cook the egg until it makes strands and waves.
5. Drop the onions into the broth and break them up with your fingers to make a pretty pattern. Serve right away.

HOT AND SOUR SOUP (SUAN LA TANG)

In China, the saying "Food is medicine" has been around for a long time. Hot and sour soup is low in calories, full of vitamins and nutrients, helps clear the lungs, warms and calms an upset stomach, and calms and clears the airways. It's a favourite meal for every day and tastes great.

INGREDIENTS:

- 4 ounces boneless pork loin, cut into
- ¼-inch-thick strips
- 1 tablespoon dark soy sauce
- 4 dried shiitake mushrooms
- 8 dried tree ear mushrooms
- 1½ tablespoons cornstarch

- ¼ cup unseasoned rice vinegar
- 2 tablespoons soy sauce
- 2 teaspoons sugar
- 1 teaspoon chilli oil (optional)
- 1 teaspoon ground white pepper
- 2 tablespoons cooking oil
- 1 peeled fresh ginger slice, about the size of a quarter
- Kosher salt 4 cups chicken broth
- 4 ounces firm tofu, rinsed and cut into
- ¼-inch strips 1 large egg, lightly beaten
- 2 scallions, both white and green parts, thinly sliced for garnish

INSTRUCTIONS:

1. In a bowl, mix the pork and dark soy sauce. Set aside.
2. Put the shiitake and tree ear mushrooms in a bowl that can handle heat and cover them with hot water. Soak for 20 minutes or until soft. Pour 14 cups of the mushroom water into a measuring cup made of glass and set it away. Drain the rest of the juice and throw it away. The shiitake mushrooms should be thinly sliced, and the tree ear mushrooms should be cut into pieces that are easy to eat. Put the bowl with the water and both kinds of mushrooms aside.
3. Mix the mushroom juice you saved with the cornstarch until there is no more. Mix vinegar, soy sauce, sugar, chilli oil (if you're using it), and white pepper. Set the sugar aside once it has dissolved.
4. Over medium-high heat, heat the oil in the wok until it shines. To make the oil taste better, add salt and ginger. Let the ginger sizzle in the oil for about 30 seconds as you move the pan around slowly. When you do this, the ginger will have a nice smell.

5. Move the pork to the pan and stir-fry it for about 3 minutes or until it is no longer pink. Take out the ginger and throw it away. Put in the soup and heat it until it boils. Add the mushrooms and turn the heat down to low. The mushrooms only need to cook for about 2 minutes. Add the tofu, stir it around, and let it cook for 2 minutes. Turn the heat back to medium-high and add the cornstarch mixture. Stir the soup for about 30 seconds or until it gets thicker. Turn down the heat so the water boils slowly.

6. Dip the fork into the beaten egg, and as you move the knife through the soup, slowly stir it with the fork. Dip the spoon into the egg and drag it through the soup to make egg threads. Once the egg has been added, let the soup simmer for a few minutes without moving so the egg threads can set.

7. Put the soup in bowls, then sprinkle the onions on top.

MOCK BIRD'S NEST SOUP (YAN WO TANG)

"Bird's nest soup" is made from a swiftlet's nest and is rare and expensive. The dried saliva is stuck to the walls of holes that don't have a bottom. In this form, the nests are made from cellophane noodles or Chinese long rice noodles.

INGREDIENTS:

- 4 ounces long rice (one bundle)
- 8 cups broth (chicken, meat, or vegetable)
- 1 tablespoon dark soy sauce
- ½ ounce dried, sliced mushrooms
- 4 ounces ground pork
- 4 ounces chopped ham
- 1 (8-ounce) can of water chestnuts, drained and chopped
- 2 large eggs, beaten

INSTRUCTIONS:

1. Cut the long rice into pieces that are 12 inches long and let them soak for 30 minutes in hot water from the tap. Drain.
2. Bring the broth to a low boil in the pan, then add the mushroom slices and soy sauce.
3. Mix in the pork, ham, water chestnuts, and long rice that has been rinsed and drained. Cook the pork for 3 or 4 minutes or until it turns brown.
4. Slowly stir the broth in one direction while dropping the eggs into the wok. Cook the eggs for about a minute or until they look like strands and waves.

CANTONESE SLOW-COOKED SOUP (LO FOH TONG)

In the slow-cooked soup, Chinese medicine and food come together. It mostly goes to the Guangdong (Canton) region in South China. Slow-cooked soup takes a long time to make, so Hong Kong and other places in South China have many chain restaurants serving it.

INGREDIENTS:

- 2 tablespoons sesame oil
- 1 tablespoon crushed fresh ginger
- 3 garlic cloves, crushed
- 1 pound ½-inch diced meat (beef, pork, chicken, lamb, or Chinese sausage)
- 1 cup carrots, roll-cut into
- ½-inch pieces (see Tip)
- 1 cup canned or frozen corn
- 4 scallions, both white and green parts, cut into ½-inch pieces
- 8 cups broth (meat, fish, or vegetable)

INSTRUCTIONS:

1. Heat the oil, ginger, and garlic in the wok until they smell good.
2. Stir-fry the meat for 2 minutes or until it is just lightly browned.
3. Stir-fry the carrots, corn, and onions for two minutes or until the food smells good.
4. Add the water and let it simmer for 2 to 4 hours until the flavours have mixed.

WINTER MELON AND PORK SOUP

Some people think that summer is an odd time for cold melon soup. It is a yin food that goes well with summer's hot and sticky weather.

INGREDIENTS:

- 8 cups broth (meat, seafood, or vegetable)
- 1 (15-ounce) can of straw mushrooms, drained and rinsed
- 8 ounces ground pork
- 1 tablespoon chopped fresh ginger
- 3 garlic cloves, crushed and chopped
- 2 tablespoons soy sauce
- 2 tablespoons Shaoxing cooking wine
- 2 cups winter melon, peeled, cored, and cut into bite-size pieces
- 4 scallions, both white and green parts, cut into ¼-inch pieces

INSTRUCTIONS:

1. Over medium heat, bring the broth and mushrooms to a slow boil in the wok.
2. Mix the pork with ginger, garlic, soy sauce, and wine in a bowl.
3. Roll the pork mixture into balls 12 inches in diameter and put them in the boiling water.
4. Put the winter melon in the broth and cook for 10 minutes or until soft.
5. Then add the onions and serve.

VEGETABLE WONTON SOUP
VEGETARIAN

In Chinese, "wonton" means "to swallow clouds." This meatless version of the classic dish is light and mild unless you add spicy sesame oil to the broth or the filling. You can give the wontons a different feel by frying them before putting them in the soup.

INGREDIENTS:

- 8 cups vegetable broth
- 1 ounce dried tree ear mushrooms
- 8 ounces extra-firm tofu, drained and crumbled
- 2 garlic cloves, crushed and chopped
- 2 tablespoons chopped fresh ginger
- 2 tablespoons hoisin sauce
- 6 scallions, both white and green parts, minced and divided
- 1 (12-ounce) package square wonton wrappers
- 2 cups sliced bok choy

INSTRUCTIONS:

1. Put the stock in the wok and bring it to a slow boil. Then add the dried mushrooms.
2. Mix the tofu with the garlic, ginger, hoisin sauce, and 2 chopped scallions in a food processor or on a cutting board.
3. Pour water into a small bowl. Put a wonton wrapper on a table to make it look like a baseball field, and sit behind home plate.
4. Place 1 teaspoon of the filling where the pitcher mound would be. Put a clean fingertip in the water and paint

around the bases. Make a triangle by folding the home plate up to the second base. Fill in what's missing.

5. Once you've made all the wontons, bring the soup to a rolling boil and add them individually.
6. After the soup has been cooking for one minute, add the sliced bok choy and cook for another minute or until the bok choy turns bright green.
7. The soup is ready to be served when the rest of the onions are added.

PROMO SOUP (YANG ROU PROMO)

The bread and lamb in this stew give it a lot of flavors flavour. People say the first Song ruler, Zhao Kuangyin, liked it the most. People know Xi'an for its promo soup and its army of clay troops.

INGREDIENTS:

- 2 tablespoons cooking oil
- 1 tablespoon chopped fresh ginger
- 3 garlic cloves, crushed and chopped
- 8 ounces ground lamb
- 1 tablespoon Chinese five-spice powder
- 1 teaspoon spicy sesame oil
- 2 tablespoons Shaoxing cooking wine
- 8 cups broth (chicken, beef, pork, or vegetable)
- 4 to 6 (6-inch) pita bread
- 4 scallions, both white and green parts, cut into ¼-inch pieces for garnishing

INSTRUCTIONS:

1. Oil should be heated on high in a wok until it shimmers.

2. Stir-fry the ginger, garlic, lamb, five-spice powder, sesame oil, and wine for two minutes or until the lamb is lightly browned and smells good.
3. Add the broth and let it cook on low for 20 minutes so that the tastes can mix.
4. For each bowl, tear up a pita into small pieces. Pour the soup over the bread.
5. When the onions are added, it's done.

TOMATO AND EGG DROP SOUP

One very popular food in Hong Kong can be made in a thousand different ways. It's also a favourite of college students who know how to cook because it only has a few specific ingredients. The basic egg drop soup tastes more umami when the tomatoes are stir-fried with oil, pepper, and wine.

INGREDIENTS:
- 2 tablespoons cooking oil
- 2 cups (1-inch diced) tomatoes
- 1 tablespoon sesame oil
- ¼ teaspoon ground white pepper
- 2 tablespoons Shaoxing cooking wine
- 8½ cups chicken or vegetable broth, divided
- ¼ cup cornstarch
- 4 large eggs, beaten
- 4 scallions, both white and green parts, cut into ¼-inch pieces

INSTRUCTIONS:
1. Oil should be heated on high in a wok until it shimmers.

2. Add the tomatoes, sesame oil, white pepper, and wine, and stir-fry for one minute or until the food smells good.
3. Turn down the heat to low and pour in 8 cups of broth.
4. In a small bowl, combine the last half cup of water with the cornstarch to make a thick paste. Add the slurry to the simmering soup and stir it for about two minutes or until it thickens and becomes clear.
5. Slowly stir the broth in one direction while dropping the eggs into the wok. Cook the eggs for about a minute or until they look like strands and waves.
6. Add the onions and serve hot or at room temperature.

MOCK SHARK FIN SOUP (YU-CHI TANG)

People used to think that shark fins could do anything from make you more sexually active to make your skin look better. A bowl can cost over $100, even though the claims haven't been proven. This one tastes better and is better for the animals.

INGREDIENTS:
- 2 ounces cellophane glass noodles
- ½ ounce sliced, dried tree ear mushrooms
- 1 teaspoon dark soy sauce
- 8½ cups broth (chicken, meat, or vegetable), divided
- ¼ cup cornstarch
- 4 ounces thinly sliced pork
- 2 crab sticks, shredded
- 2 large eggs, beaten

INSTRUCTIONS:

1. Soak the cellophane noodles in hot water from the faucet for 15 minutes.
2. Put the sliced mushrooms, dark soy sauce, and broth in the pan and bring them to a low simmer.
3. Make a slurry by mixing the last half cup of broth with the cornstarch in a small bowl. Stir it into the water until it thickens and becomes clearer.
4. Add the pork to the water and cook for one minute or until it's done. Shred the crab sticks and add those, too.
5. When the noodles are soft, cut them into 2-inch pieces and put them in the soup.
6. As you slowly pour the eggs into the wok, stir the broth in one way. About a minute should be enough time to cook the egg until it makes strands and waves.

BEEF, PORK, AND LAMB

SICHUAN BEEF

This stir-fry is easy to make during the week. It has chopped beef and a sweet and spicy sauce. It goes well with other foods to make a full meal. The julienned carrots make the dish sweet and crunchy. Sichuan food is usually spicy, but you can decide how much chile goes into this dish.

INGREDIENTS:

For the marinade
- 2 teaspoons cornstarch
- 1 teaspoon sesame oil
- 1 teaspoon soy sauce
- 1 pound beef tenderloin or sirloin cut into
- ¼-inch strips (like French fries) For the sauce
- 1 tablespoon soy sauce
- 1 teaspoon brown sugar
- 1 teaspoon sesame oil
- 1 teaspoon chilli oil
- ½ tablespoon oyster sauce
- ¼ teaspoon dark soy sauce
- For the stir-fry
- 2 tablespoons cooking oil
- 2 garlic cloves, minced
- 5 or 6 dried red chiles
- ½ carrot, julienned

- 1 scallion, both white and green parts, chopped for garnish
- To make the marinade

INSTRUCTIONS:

1. Mix the cornstarch, olive oil, and soy sauce in a small bowl. Add the ground beef and mix. Just 15 minutes at room temperature is all you need. To make the sauce,
2. Mix the dark soy sauce, the oyster sauce, the dark soy sauce, the sesame oil, the chilli oil, and the brown sugar in a small bowl. Set it aside. How to make stir-fried food
3. Over medium-high heat, heat the oil in the wok until it shines.
4. Stir-fry the meat for about 30 seconds or until it is medium-rare.
5. After adding the garlic, stir-fry the beef for another minute until it is almost done. Mix the sauce and dried red chiles with the other ingredients.
6. Take the dish off the heat and stir in the carrots.
7. Place the beef on a plate and add the onions on top.

INSTANT HOISIN BEEF AND PEPPER

This quick stir-fry uses thinly sliced rib-eye steak, which is used to make Philly cheesesteaks. If you want to cut the steak yourself, putting it in the freezer for 30 minutes helps. Hoisin sauce and chilli peppers give food flavour and heat.

INGREDIENTS:

- 1 pound shaved rib-eye steak, cut across the grain into 2-inch pieces
- 1 tablespoon cornstarch
- 1 tablespoon Shaoxing cooking wine
- 1 tablespoon soy sauce
- 1 tablespoon toasted sesame oil
- 2 tablespoons cooking oil
- 1 tablespoon chopped fresh ginger
- 2 garlic cloves, crushed and chopped
- 1 red bell pepper, cut into
- 1-inch pieces
- ¼ cup hoisin sauce
- 4 scallions, both white and green parts, cut into
- 1-inch pieces for garnishing
- Rice or noodles for serving

INSTRUCTIONS:

1. Mix the steak, cornstarch, wine, soy sauce, and sesame oil in a big bowl.
2. Oil should be heated on high in a wok until it shimmers.
3. Stir-fry the ginger, garlic, and bell pepper for 1 minute or until they smell good.
4. Stir-fry the steak for one minute or until it's medium-rare.

5. After adding the hoisin sauce, Stir-fry for 1 minute, or until the steak is cooked. The green onions can be used to decorate a dish. Serve over noodles or rice.

THAI LEMON PEPPER BEEF WITH CARROTS, PEANUTS, AND SCALLIONS

This quick and easy stir-fry has a nice citrus zing from the grated lemon peel and spicy sesame oil. Carrots and onions add sweetness and crunch to the dish.

INGREDIENTS:

- 1 pound thin-cut sirloin steak, cut into
- ¼-inch strips across the grain
- 1 teaspoon spicy sesame oil
- 1 tablespoon soy sauce
- 1 tablespoon Shaoxing cooking wine
- 1 teaspoon fish sauce
- ¼ cup plus
- 1 tablespoon cornstarch divided
- 2 tablespoons cooking oil
- 1 tablespoon chopped fresh ginger
- 2 garlic cloves, crushed and chopped
- 1 medium carrot, roll-cut into
- ½-inch pieces (1 cup)
- 1 medium red bell pepper, cut into
- 1-inch pieces of Grated zest and juice of 2 lemons
- ¼ cup brown sugar
- ½ cup chopped peanuts

Sell your books at
World of Books!
Go to sell.worldofbooks.com
and get an instant price
quote. We even pay the
shipping - see what your old
books are worth today!

Inspected By: Fernando_Mendez

0008407051 4

- 4 scallions, both white and green parts, cut into 1-inch pieces of Rice or noodles for serving

INSTRUCTIONS:

1. Mix the meat, sesame oil, soy sauce, wine, fish sauce, and 1/4 cup of cornstarch in a medium bowl.
2. Oil for cooking should be heated in a pan until it smokes over high heat.
3. Stir-fry the ginger, garlic, and carrot for 1 minute or until they smell good.
4. Stir-fry the steak for one minute or until it's medium-rare.
5. Stir-fry the bell pepper for one minute or until it smells good.
6. Stir-fry for one minute to mix the lemon zest, juice, brown sugar, and last tablespoon of cornstarch.
7. Add the peanuts and onions and stir until everything is mixed well. Serve over rice or noodles.

DRY-FRIED BEEF (GAN BIAN NIU ROU)

China doesn't eat a lot of beef because it's very expensive to raise and buy cattle. But the result is wonderful when Chinese cooking methods, like a good stir-fry and a few key spices, are used to cook beef. Serve this easy stir-fry with warmed rice to make a filling meal. It tastes good because of the umami and the black beans.

INGREDIENTS:

- 8 ounces sirloin or rib-eye steak
- 2 tablespoons Shaoxing cooking wine or dry sherry
- 1 tablespoon soy sauce

- 1 teaspoon potato starch ½ teaspoon sugar
- 2 teaspoons fermented black beans
- 4 tablespoons cooking oil
- 1 teaspoon Sichuan peppercorns
- 2 garlic cloves, minced
- 1 (1-inch) piece fresh ginger, minced
- 5 dried red chiles, torn in half
- 1 tablespoon chilli oil
- 4 ounces of fresh bean sprouts
- 1 tablespoon dark soy sauce
- 2 scallions, both white and green parts, finely chopped

INSTRUCTIONS:

1. Cut the beef into strips that are 2 inches long and as thin as you can make them. Try making something that looks like sprouted beans.
2. Mix the wine, soy sauce, potato starch, and sugar in a small bowl. Set aside.
3. Soak the fermented black beans in warm water for 5 minutes in a small bowl, then drain them and chop them very finely. Set aside.
4. Over medium heat, heat the oil in the pot until it shines.
5. Stir-fry the Sichuan peppercorns for about 15 seconds or until they smell good. Take the peppercorns out with a forked spoon and throw them away. Turn the heat up to high (until you see smoke), add the beef, and stir-fry it for 2 minutes. Put the meat in a medium bowl with a colander over it. Don't throw it away.
6. Put the two tablespoons of oil you took out back into the wok and heat it. Stir-fry the garlic and ginger until they smell good, which should take about 10 seconds. Stir-fry for 1 minute after adding the dried chiles, chilli oil, fermented black beans, bean sprouts, and dark soy sauce.

7. Put the meat back in the wok and stir-fry it for one more minute. After adding the wine sauce blend, Stir-fry for about a minute, or until most of the sauce is gone.
8. Stir in the green onions. Prepare hot.

MA PO TOFU

If you buy a packet of Ma Po Tofu instant sauce in the Asian food area of a Western supermarket to put on your hamburger meat, it won't be the same as real Ma Po Dou Fu. Sichuan peppercorn is a magical spice. It takes away the pain of the heat from the chiles and makes your nose and mouth smell and taste like wood, pine, and flowers. This traditional dish goes well with steamed rice.

INGREDIENTS:

- 2 tablespoons cooking oil
- 8 ounces lean ground pork
- 3 tablespoons doubanjiang (Chinese chilli bean paste)
- 2 tablespoons fermented black beans
- 1 teaspoon red pepper flakes
- 1 tablespoon dark soy sauce
- 1 cup chicken broth
- 1 (14-ounce) container of firm tofu, cut into 1-inch cubes
- 1 teaspoon peeled fresh ginger, minced
- 2 tablespoons cold water
- 1 teaspoon potato starch
- 1 teaspoon freshly ground
- Sichuan peppercorns
- 1 scallion, green part only, chopped, for garnish

INSTRUCTIONS:

1. Heat the oil in the pot over medium-high heat until it shines.
2. Stir-fry the pork until it falls apart into small pieces. Mix black beans, red pepper flakes, soy sauce, and water in the doubanjiang. Stir-fry the tofu and ginger for 1 minute, careful not to break up the tofu. Turn down the heat and let the food simmer for 5 minutes so the tastes can mix.
3. Mix the cold water and potato starch in a small bowl. Turn the heat up to medium-high and add the mixture of water and starch. Stir-fry for one minute, and then take it off the heat.
4. Add the ground Sichuan peppercorns and the onion to make it look nice. Prepare hot.

BEEF AND BROCCOLI

Tender, spicy broccoli beef over steamed rice will do the job when you want Chinese food. The amount of sweet hoisin sauce and salty oyster sauce is just right. They get soft when you put beef strips in baking soda before you cook them.

INGREDIENTS:
- 12 ounces skirt steak, cut across the grain into
- ¼-inch-thick slices
- 1 tablespoon baking soda
- 1 tablespoon cornstarch
- 4 tablespoons water divided
- 2 tablespoons oyster sauce
- 2 tablespoons Shaoxing cooking wine
- 2 teaspoons light brown sugar
- 1 tablespoon hoisin sauce
- 2 tablespoons cooking oil

- 4 fresh ginger slices, about the size of a quarter Kosher salt
- 1 pound broccoli, cut into bite-size florets
- 2 garlic cloves, finely minced

INSTRUCTIONS:

1. Mix the beef and baking soda in a small bowl to cover the meat. Set aside for 10 minutes. Rinse the meat well, and then use paper towels to dry it.
2. In another small bowl, mix 2 tablespoons of water with the flour. Then, mix the oyster sauce, brown sugar, wine, and hoisin sauce. Set aside.
3. Heat the oil in the pot over medium-high heat until it shines. To make the oil taste better, add salt and ginger. Stir the ginger in the oil while it sizzles for about 30 seconds. Stir-fry the meat for 3–4 minutes or until it's no longer pink. Put the meat in a bowl and set it away.
4. Broccoli and garlic should be stir-fried for one minute. After adding the last two tablespoons of water, stir-fry for another minute. Cover the wok and steam the broccoli for 6–8 minutes or until it is just crisp-tender.
5. Return the beef to the wok and stir in the sauce for 2 or 3 minutes until the meat is completely covered and the sauce thickens. The mixture should be served hot on a plate.

RED COOKED PORK (HONG SHAO ROU)

People say that Chairman Mao's favourite meal is this easy and tasty roasted pork belly. The Chinese name means "red-cooked pork" because the pork is spiced up while cooking.

INGREDIENTS:

- 1 pound pork belly or shoulder, cut into 1-inch pieces
- 2 tablespoons cooking oil
- 4 garlic cloves, crushed and chopped
- ¼ cup sugar
- ¼ cup Shaoxing cooking wine
- 3 tablespoons soy sauce
- 1 tablespoon
- Chinese five-spice powder
- Steamed rice for serving

INSTRUCTIONS:

1. Put the pork in the pan and turn the heat to medium-high. Bring up to a boil just enough water to cover the pork. Cook for 15 minutes and remove any foam that comes to the top.
2. Take out the pork and strain it. The soup can stay.
3. Put the oil, garlic, and sugar into the wok and heat them on high for about a minute or until the sugar goes brown. Stir-fry the pork for two or three minutes until it turns brown.
4. Add the reserved soup, wine, soy sauce, and five-spice powder. Over medium heat, let the pork simmer for 45 minutes or until it is soft. Stir the pork occasionally to keep it from sticking to the bottom of the pan.

5. Add to cooked rice.

PORK RIBS WITH BLACK BEAN SAUCE (DAO SEE PAI GOUT)

A favourite dim sum dish is steamed pork ribs with black bean sauce. We're taking the idea to the next level by stir-frying the ribs in a pan and cooking them in a tasty sauce. Serve with white rice or brown rice that has been warmed.

INGREDIENTS:

For the marinade
- 2 teaspoons Shaoxing cooking wine
- 2 teaspoons cornstarch
- ½ teaspoon salt Pinch ground white pepper
- 2 pounds pork ribs, cut into
- 1½-inch pieces For the sauce
- 1½ cups water
- 2 tablespoons black bean sauce
- 2 teaspoons sugar
- 2 teaspoons soy sauce
- 1 teaspoon dark soy sauce For the stir-fry
- 2 tablespoons cooking oil
- 1-inch piece of ginger, peeled and minced
- 2 garlic cloves, minced
- 1 scallion, both white and green parts, chopped for garnish
- To make the marinade

INSTRUCTIONS:

1. Mix the wine, cornstarch, salt, and white pepper in a small bowl. Add the pork and stir it in. Let it sit out for about 20 minutes at room temperature. To make the sauce,
2. Mix the water, black bean sauce, sugar, soy sauce, and dark soy sauce in a small bowl. Set it aside. How to make stir-fried food
3. Heat the oil in the pot over medium-high heat until it shines.
4. Spread the ribs marinating out in one layer in the wok. Let them cook for 30 seconds without being stirred. Add the ginger and garlic, then flip the ribs with a wok spoon.
5. For about 2 minutes, or until the food goes brown, stir it every 10 seconds. Put the lid on the pan, add the sauce, and stir.
6. Turn down the heat and cook it for about 20 minutes. Check on the sauce every few minutes to make sure it's not going too quickly. If it's already boiling, keep it at a low boil by adding water as needed.
7. Put the ribs on a plate to serve, then put the onions on top. Serve right away.

SPICY POACHED BEEF (SHUI ZHU NIU ROU)

This tasty, spicy dish is very popular in the Chinese region of Sichuan. "Beef boiled in water" is what the name means. Velveting the beef in advance helps make it tender.

INGREDIENTS:

- 1 pound thin-sliced sirloin steak, cut across the grain
- 1 teaspoon spicy sesame oil
- 1 tablespoon Chinese five-spice powder
- 1 tablespoon soy sauce
- 1 tablespoon Shaoxing cooking wine
- 1 tablespoon oyster sauce
- ¼ cup plus
- 1 tablespoon cornstarch divided
- 2 tablespoons cooking oil
- 1 tablespoon chopped fresh ginger
- 3 garlic cloves, crushed and chopped
- 2 cups Gai Lan (Chinese broccoli), cut into
- 2-inch pieces
- 2 cups broth (meat, seafood, or vegetable)
- 1 (15-ounce) can of straw mushrooms, drained and rinsed
- 4 scallions, both white and green parts, cut into ¼-inch pieces for garnishing

INSTRUCTIONS:

1. Mix the steak, sesame oil, five-spice powder, soy sauce, wine, oyster sauce, and 1/4 cup of cornstarch.
2. Oil should be heated on high in a wok until it shimmers.

3. Stir-fry the ginger, garlic, and gai lan for 1 minute or until the smell is good.
4. Turn down the heat to a boil and add the broth and mushrooms.
5. Again, stir the steak to ensure it's well covered, then add it to the simmering water.
6. Let the steak cook for two minutes, then add the last tablespoon of cornstarch to make it a little thicker.
7. Serve over rice or noodles and top with onions.

SESAME BEEF AND BOK CHOY

This easy stir-fry has a mild, nutty taste from the Chinese sesame paste, wine, and soy sauce. Sesame paste can be replaced with tahini, but it doesn't have the same strong taste.

INGREDIENTS:

- 8 ounces thin-cut sirloin steak, sliced into
- ⅛-inch pieces across the grain
- 2 tablespoons Shaoxing cooking wine
- 2 tablespoons soy sauce
- 1 teaspoon spicy sesame oil
- 1 teaspoon sesame paste
- 1 tablespoon cornstarch
- 2 tablespoons cooking oil
- 1 tablespoon chopped fresh ginger
- 2 garlic cloves, crushed and chopped
- 1 red bell pepper, diced into ½-inch pieces
- 2 cups bok choy, sliced into ½-inch pieces
- ¼ cup water

- 4 scallions, both white and green parts, cut into ¼-inch pieces for garnishing
- 1 tablespoon toasted sesame seeds for garnishing
- Rice or noodles for serving

INSTRUCTIONS:

1. Steak, wine, soy sauce, sesame oil, paste, and cornstarch should all be mixed in a bowl.
2. Oil should be heated on high in a wok until it shimmers.
3. Stir-fry the steak, ginger, and garlic for one minute or until the steak smells good.
4. Stir the pepper and bok choy for a minute or until the steak is medium-rare.
5. Add the water and stir until a glaze forms, which should take about a minute.
6. Serve over rice or noodles and sprinkle with onions and sesame seeds.

GINGER BEEF WITH ORANGE CARROTS

It sounds easy to cook beef with ginger, but aren't carrots already sweet? This dish also discusses how fresh orange juice and rind taste sweet and sour.

INGREDIENTS:

- 8 ounces thin-cut sirloin steak, sliced into
- ⅛-inch pieces across the grain
- 2 tablespoons Shaoxing cooking wine
- 2 tablespoons soy sauce
- 1 teaspoon spicy sesame oil
- Grated zest and juice of 1 orange, juice divided

- 2 tablespoons cornstarch, divided
- 2 tablespoons cooking oil
- 1 tablespoon chopped ginger
- 2 garlic cloves, crushed and chopped
- 1 cup (½-inch) roll-cut carrots
- 1 medium onion, diced into
- 1-inch pieces
- 4 scallions, both white and green parts, sliced into ¼-inch pieces for garnishing
- 1 tablespoon toasted sesame seeds for garnishing
- Rice or noodles for serving

INSTRUCTIONS:

1. Mix the steak, wine, soy sauce, sesame oil, orange zest, half orange juice, and 1 tablespoon of cornstarch. Blend well.
2. Oil should be heated on high in a wok until it shimmers.
3. Stir-fry the ginger, garlic, and carrots for 2 minutes or until they smell good.
4. Stir-fry the steak and onion for one minute or until the meat is medium-rare.
5. Add the last tablespoon of flour and the rest of the orange juice. Stir for about one minute or until a glaze forms.
6. Serve over rice or noodles and sprinkle with onions and sesame seeds.

STEAMED PORK RIBS WITH BLACK BEAN SAUCE AND CHILES

When pork ribs are steamed, they get juicy, soft, and full of taste. By chopping the bones in half and pulling them apart, you can get to the collagen in the bone marrow, which tastes good for your bones, joints, and skin.

INGREDIENTS:

- 1-pound baby back ribs, separated and cut in half (1 to 2 inches long)
- 2 tablespoons black bean sauce
- 1 tablespoon Shaoxing cooking wine
- 1 tablespoon cornstarch
- 4 dried chiles, chopped
- 1 teaspoon spicy sesame oil
- 1 tablespoon chopped fresh ginger
- 4 garlic cloves, crushed and chopped

INSTRUCTIONS:

1. Mix the ribs, black bean sauce, wine, cornstarch, chiles, sesame oil, ginger, and garlic in a big bowl. Combine all the parts. Put in a pie pan or other flat-bottomed dish.
2. Bring an inch of water to a boil in the pan over high heat. Put a rack and a shelf in the wok. Cover it and let it steam for 20 minutes or until it's done. If the fire dies down, add more water.

SICHUAN CUMIN LAMB STIR-FRY WITH SWEET POTATOES (ZI RAN YANG ROU)

People in Sichuan like to eat lamb and eat it often. Spain sent sweet potatoes to China in the 1500s. They go well with foods with a lot of fat, like lamb. It tastes great when something is both sweet and spicy.

INGREDIENTS:

- 8 ounces boneless leg of lamb, sliced into
- ¼-inch pieces across the grain
- 1 tablespoon soy sauce
- 1 tablespoon
- Shaoxing cooking wine
- 1 teaspoon spicy sesame oil
- ¼ cup cornstarch
- 2 tablespoons cooking oil
- 1 tablespoon chopped fresh ginger
- 3 garlic cloves, crushed and chopped
- 2 cups sweet potato julienned into matchstick-sized pieces
- 1 medium onion, cut into ½-inch pieces
- 1 tablespoon ground cumin
- 1 teaspoon red pepper flakes
- 1 teaspoon Chinese five-spice powder
- ¼ teaspoon ground
- Sichuan peppercorns
- 4 scallions, cut into
- ¼-inch pieces of Rice or noodles for serving

INSTRUCTIONS:

1. Mix the lamb, soy sauce, wine, olive oil, and cornstarch in a medium bowl to coat.
2. Oil should be heated on high in a wok until it shimmers.
3. Stir-fry the ginger, garlic, and sweet potato for 1 minute or until they smell good.
4. Stir-fry the onions for one minute or until they smell good.
5. Stir-fry the lamb for one minute or until it is medium-rare.
6. Stir-fry the cumin, red pepper flakes, five-spice powder, and Sichuan peppercorns for one minute or until the mixture smells good.
7. Serve over rice or noodles and top with onions.

THAI CURRY LAMB MEATBALLS

The spicy taste of these deep-fried meatballs comes from red Thai curry. They are served with a sweet and sour coconut lime sauce. I'm getting hungry just thinking about these on rice, noodles, or in a soft sub roll.

INGREDIENTS:

- 1 pound ground lamb
- 1 medium onion, minced
- ¼ cup panko bread crumbs
- ¼ cup red Thai curry paste
- 1 tablespoon fish sauce
- 2 cups oil for deep-frying
- 1 (13½-ounce) can of coconut milk divided
- 2 tablespoons brown sugar

- Grated zest and juice of 1 lime
- 2 tablespoons cornstarch
- Chopped fresh cilantro for garnish

INSTRUCTIONS:

1. Mix the meat, onion, panko bread crumbs, curry paste, and fish sauce in a medium bowl. Make between 12 and 16 meatballs about the size of a bite.
2. When the oil in the wok hits 325 degrees Fahrenheit, deep-fry the meatballs for 4 to 6 minutes or until golden brown. The water has to go somewhere.
3. Take off the paper and put the meatballs back in the wok. Put all the brown sugar and coconut milk except for 1/4 cup in the wok. Bring slowly to a boil.
4. Mix the cornstarch and the 1/4 cup of coconut milk you saved in a small bowl. Mix into the sweet-and-sour sauce already boiling, and cook for 2 minutes or until the sauce gets thicker. Pour the sauce over the meatballs in bowls and sprinkle the mint.

FIVE-SPICE STEAMED LAMB AND CABBAGE

Ground lamb that has been cooked and is well-seasoned doesn't need any extra oil to stay moist and tender. So, it's both tasty and good for you. With steamed rice, the chopped cabbage, fragrant ingredients, five-spice seasoning, and natural juices make a tasty meal.

INGREDIENTS:

- 8 ounces ground lamb
- 2 cups chopped
- Chinese cabbage (bok choy or napa)
- 1 tablespoon chopped fresh ginger
- 3 garlic cloves, crushed and chopped
- 1 teaspoon spicy sesame oil
- 1 tablespoon Chinese five-spice powder
- ¼ cup soy sauce
- 3 large eggs, scrambled
- Steamed rice for serving

INSTRUCTIONS:

1. Mix the lamb, cabbage, ginger, garlic, sesame oil, five-spice powder, soy sauce, and eggs in a big bowl. Put in a pie pan or other flat-bottomed dish.
2. Bring an inch of water to a boil in the pan over high heat. Put a rack in the pot and the pan on the frame. Cover it and let it steam for 10 minutes or until it's done.
3. Add to cooked rice.

BRAISED BEEF AND DAIKON RADISH

This is the best comfort food from China. Think of it as a Chinese beef stew with soft, creamy root vegetables and tender pieces of meat in a rich broth. Yum!

INGREDIENTS:

- 2 tablespoons cooking oil
- 1 pound stew beef, cut into 1-inch pieces
- 2 tablespoons chopped fresh ginger
- 3 garlic cloves, crushed and chopped
- 1 cup Shaoxing cooking wine
- 2 tablespoons dark soy sauce
- 1 tablespoon Chinese five-spice powder
- 4 cups water divided
- 2 cups daikon radish, cut into 1-inch cubes

INSTRUCTIONS:

1. Heat the oil in the pot on high until it starts to crackle.
2. Stir-fry the beef, ginger, and garlic for two minutes or until the meat is cooked.
3. Pour the wine, dark soy sauce, five-spice powder, and one cup of water into the pan and bring to a boil.
4. Turn down the heat to a simmer for one hour. Every few minutes, stir the food so it doesn't stick and burn.
5. Add the radish that has been cut up and the last 3 cups of water. Let the daikon cook for 30 minutes or until it's soft. Serve on rice, noodles, or by itself.

STEAMED BEEF WITH BLACK BEANS AND SUGAR SNAP PEAS

This is a healthy way to make beef that is tender, juicy, and full of taste. When you add steamed vegetables that have been browned, the meal gets a great taste, colour, texture, and nutrition.

INGREDIENTS:

- 8 ounces of ground beef
- 2 tablespoons black bean sauce
- 2 tablespoons Shaoxing cooking wine
- 1 tablespoon soy sauce
- 1 tablespoon toasted sesame oil
- 2 dozen fresh sugar snap peas
- Rice or noodles for serving

INSTRUCTIONS:

1. Mix the ground beef, black bean sauce, wine, soy sauce, and sesame oil in a big bowl.
2. Spread the mixture in a thin layer in a pie pan or other dish. Put the peas on top of the beef.
3. Bring an inch of water to a boil in the pan over high heat. Put a rack and a shelf in the wok. Cover it and let it steam for 10 minutes or until it's done.
4. Serve over noodles or rice.

CHINESE AROMATIC HONEY PORK AND STRAW MUSHROOMS

This quick and easy stir-fry starts with ginger, garlic, and onions from Cantonese cooking. This dish's green mushrooms and soy sauce give it an umami flavour. It goes well on rice or noodles that have been warmed.

INGREDIENTS:

- 1 pound ground pork
- 1 tablespoon Shaoxing cooking wine
- 1 tablespoon honey
- 1 teaspoon spicy sesame oil
- 2 tablespoons cooking oil
- 1 tablespoon chopped fresh ginger
- 2 garlic cloves, crushed and chopped
- 1 (15-ounce) can of straw mushrooms, drained and rinsed
- 2 tablespoons soy sauce
- 4 scallions, both white and green parts, cut into ¼-inch pieces
- Rice or noodles for serving

INSTRUCTIONS:

1. Mix the pork, wine, honey, and sesame oil in a bowl.
2. Oil should be heated on high in a wok until it shimmers.
3. Stir-fry the pork, ginger, and garlic for 2 minutes or until it smells good and turns brown.
4. Stir-fry the mushrooms and soy sauce for one minute or until everything is well mixed.
5. Stir-fry the onions for one minute or until everything is well mixed.

6. Serve over noodles or rice.

LAPSANG SOUCHONG TEA-SMOKED PORK RIBS

Lapsang Souchong tea adds a smelly, smoky flavour to stewed pork ribs. Farmers in Fujian's Wuyi Mountains made this tea by drying the leaves over wood fires to get them to market faster. You will need a piece of metal foil to keep the things you want to smoke in the wok.

INGREDIENTS:

- 1 pound baby back pork ribs, separated and cut in half (1 to 2 inches long)
- ¼ cup thick soy sauce
- ¼ cup lapsang souchong tea leaves
- ¼ cup brown sugar
- ¼ cup uncooked long-grain white rice
- 1 tablespoon Chinese five-spice powder
- ¼ cup cooking oil
- 1 tablespoon ginger, crushed and chopped
- 4 garlic cloves, crushed and chopped
- ¼ cup ketchup
- 1 tablespoon dark soy sauce
- 1 teaspoon spicy sesame oil
- In a large bowl, combine the ribs and soy sauce.

INSTRUCTIONS:

1. Mix the tea leaves, brown sugar, rice, and five-spice powder on a square piece of aluminium foil. Make a shallow saucer about 12 inches deep by rolling up the

ends. It should have an open top. Put the paper plate in the wok's bottom.

2. Put a rack in the middle of the work. Place the ribs on a shelf or a plate that can take the heat. Use a lid with a cap to cover the wok.
3. If you're cooking inside, open any windows near the stove and turn up the speed of your vent fan. If you can't get the air out of the room, do the following steps outside.
4. Turn the heat up to high, and turn it down to medium when the work starts to bubble. Don't take the top off! Let the ribs smoke for 10 minutes on medium heat, then turn off the heat and let them smoke for another 10 minutes.
5. Move the ribs to a bowl and remove the paper you used to smoke them.
6. Put the oil in the wok and heat it high until it shatters.
7. Stir-fry the ginger, garlic, and ribs for two minutes or until the food smells good.
8. After adding the ketchup, dark soy sauce, and sesame oil, stir-fry the meat for 2 minutes, or until it is well done.

PEKING PORK RIBS (CAPITAL RIBS, JING DU PAI GU)

This dish is interesting because it didn't come from Peking (Beijing) but from Jing Du, which is in the city of Nanjing in the south. When the city moved north to Peking, the name changed, but the recipe didn't. Still not sure? No matter what you call them, these ribs are tasty.

INGREDIENTS:

- 1 pound baby back pork ribs, separated and cut in half (1 to 2 inches long)
- 2 tablespoons Shaoxing cooking wine
- 1 tablespoon brown sugar
- ¼ cup cornstarch Oil for deep-frying
- 1 tablespoon chopped fresh ginger
- 4 garlic cloves, crushed and chopped
- ¼ cup ketchup
- 1 teaspoon spicy sesame oil
- 1 tablespoon dark soy sauce

INSTRUCTIONS:

1. Mix the ribs, wine, brown sugar, and cornstarch in a big bowl until all the ribs are evenly coated.
2. Heat about 2 inches of oil in the wok until it hits 325°F or until you can make bubbles with a wooden chopstick.
3. Fry the ribs in oil until golden brown, then let them cool on a rack or some paper towels.
4. All but 1 tablespoon of the oil should be taken out of the pot, and the ginger and garlic should be lightly browned.

5. Stir-fry the ribs for 2 minutes, ensuring the ketchup, sesame oil, and dark soy sauce are spread out evenly. Prepare hot.

CHICKEN AND DUCK

CRISPY CHICKEN AND RED CHILES

When I order this dish at a Chinese restaurant, I often spend too much time looking for the chicken pieces among the big lantern chiles and a sea of bitter Sichuan peppercorns. When you make this dish at home, you won't skimp on the chicken, making it much better. The peppercorns kick the word, and the toasty heat of the chiles goes well with it without overpowering it.

INGREDIENTS:

For the chicken
- 2 pounds chicken, cut into
- 1-inch pieces
- 3 tablespoons Shaoxing cooking wine or dry sherry
- 3 tablespoons dark soy sauce
- 1 cup potato starch
- 1 tablespoon freshly ground
- Sichuan peppercorns
- 1 tablespoon ground red chilli powder or cayenne pepper
- 2 teaspoons sea salt
- Cooking oil for deep-frying

For the sauce
- 10 garlic cloves, sliced
- 1 teaspoon freshly ground Sichuan peppercorns
- 3 tablespoons doubanjiang (Chinese chilli bean paste)
- 2 tablespoons minced fresh ginger
- 1 cup dried red chiles

- ¼ teaspoon sea salt

INSTRUCTIONS:

1. For the chicken to
2. Mix the chicken, wine, and soy sauce in a big bowl. Toss the chicken around to coat it, then set it away while you finish the rest of the dish.
3. Mix the potato starch, ground Sichuan peppercorns, chile powder, and salt in a small, shallow bowl.
4. Take a few chicken pieces out of the marinade, shake off any extra sauce, and roll the chicken in the spiced starch mixture. Place on a plate.
5. Heat 2 inches of oil in the pot until it sparkles over high heat. Fry the chicken until golden brown, which should take about 10 minutes.
6. Fry the chicken in two or three batches to cook evenly on all sides. When the chicken is done, put it on a plate covered with paper towels. When you're done frying all the chicken, pour the extra oil into a jar or bowl that can handle heat. In the pan, put 3 tablespoons of oil. To make the sauce,
7. Put the oil in the wok and heat it high until it shatters.
8. Stir-fry the garlic for about ten seconds or until it smells good. Stir-fry the doubanjiang, ginger, and Sichuan peppercorn powder until the sauce turns red.
9. Bring the chicken back to the pan and toss it in the sauce to cover it.
   After adding the dried red chiles and salt, stir-fry for 2 minutes. Serve hot.

CASHEW CHICKEN

This dish was first made by David Leong of Springfield, Missouri, in 1963. It made enough money for him to open a restaurant, which he ran until 1999. In 2010, Leong's son opened his diner. A lot of people still likes cashew chicken. Here's one you can make at home that is fresh and tasty.

INGREDIENTS:

- 2 tablespoons vegetable oil
- 3 garlic cloves, crushed and chopped
- 1 tablespoon crushed and chopped fresh ginger
- 1 medium carrot, roll-cut into ½-inch pieces
- 1 pound boneless chicken thighs, cut into
- 1-inch cubes
- 1 medium onion, halved and cut into ½-inch slices
- 1 red bell pepper, diced into ½-inch pieces
- 1 cup dry-roasted cashews
- 1 cup chopped bok choy (about ½-inch reports)
- 4 tablespoons soy sauce
- 2 tablespoons honey
- 1 tablespoon toasted sesame oil
- 1 teaspoon cornstarch
- 1 bunch (6 to 8) scallions, cut into
- ½-inch pieces of Steamed rice for serving

INSTRUCTIONS:

1. Put the oil in the wok and heat it high until it shatters.
2. Stir-fry the carrot, garlic, and ginger for 1 minute. Stir-fry the chicken and onion for 1 minute. Stir-fry for 1 minute after adding the bell pepper and nuts. In a stir-fry, cook the bok choy for 1 minute.

3. Mix the soy sauce, honey, sesame oil, and cornstarch in a small bowl. Put the sauce in the pan and stir it for about two minutes until a glaze forms.
4. Put an end to the cooking and then add the onions.
5. Add to cooked rice.

VARIATION: You can substitute 1 cup of chopped zucchini for the bok choy.

CRISPY STEAMED DUCK

Peking duck is an old and well-known dish from China. Since the beginning, chefs who know how to make this dish have served it in restaurants. The roasted duck is served with thin pancakes, sliced onions, and hoisin sauce. The duck is cut up at the table. Duck is known to have a lot of fat in it. When you steam the breast before you fry it, most of the fat melts away, and the heart stays soft.

INGREDIENTS:
- 4 boneless, skin-on duck breasts
- 2 tablespoons cornstarch
- 1 tablespoon
- Chinese five-spice powder
- 5 scallions, both white and green parts, sliced
- Steamed rice, noodles, or pancakes for serving
- Hoisin sauce for dipping
- Score the duck skin with shallow crosscuts about ¼ inch apart.

INSTRUCTIONS:
1. Set the wok or a pot with a steamer basket over high heat. Fill the basket with water until it's 1 inch from the

bottom. Put the duck in the basket with the skin down when the water starts to boil. Cover and steam for 10 minutes or until almost all the water is gone. Take the duck and steamer basket out of the pot, but don't pour out the rest of the juice.

2. Turn the heat to medium and cook for 3 minutes more to remove the last bit of water.
3. Put the duck, the cornstarch, and the five-spice powder in a big bag with a zipper. Spend 2 minutes rubbing your back.
4. The duck fat should be shiny when cooked over medium-high heat. Fry the duck for 1 minute with the skin side up. Fry the duck for 2 minutes or until the skin is brown and crisp.
5. Cut the duck into thin strips or cubes, sprinkle it with onions, and serve it with steamed rice, noodles, pancakes, and hoisin sauce to dip.

THREE-COLOR SHREDDED CHICKEN (SAN SI JI DIANA)

This quick and easy stir-fry has three colours because it has onions, ginger, and garlic. It's not hard to learn how to cook Chinese food, even if you've never done it before. For the traditional way, you can use lettuce instead of bell pepper. Celtuce is a veggie that looks like lettuce and is liked for its long stalk.

INGREDIENTS:

For the marinade
- 2 boneless, skinless chicken breasts

- 1 large egg white, beaten
- 1 tablespoon potato starch
- 1 tablespoon water
- 1 teaspoon Shaoxing cooking wine or dry sherry
- 1 teaspoon sea salt

For the stir-fry

- 2 tablespoons cooking oil
- 1 scallion, both white and green parts, finely chopped
- 1 (1-inch) piece peeled fresh ginger, minced
- 2 garlic cloves, minced
- 1 cup julienned green bell pepper
- 1 cup julienned carrot
- 1 tablespoon Shaoxing cooking wine or dry sherry
- 1 teaspoon sugar
- 1 teaspoon sea salt
- ½ teaspoon ground white pepper
- To make the marinade

INSTRUCTIONS:

1. If you put the chicken in the freezer for 15 minutes, it will be easier to cut. Then, cut the chicken into slices and cut each piece into strips that are 1/4 inch wide.
2. Mix the egg white, potato starch, 1 tablespoon of water, wine, and salt in a medium bowl. To cover the chicken, stir it around. Let the chicken sit in the marinade while you prepare the other things. How to make stir-fried food
3. Put the oil in the wok and heat it on high until it shatters. Stir-fry the chicken pieces for about a minute or until they fall apart.
4. Stir-fry for 1 minute after adding the onion, ginger, and garlic. Add the carrot and bell pepper. Add the sugar, salt, white pepper, and wine to the pan. For 2 minutes, stir-fry the food.

5. Put the chicken on a serving plate and serve it while it is still hot.

FIVE-SPICE ORANGE DUCK MEATBALLS

Meatballs that taste great are made with orange peel and a strong five-spice blend. Glaze them with an orange ketchup-hoisin sauce that is easy to make, and they will go quickly.

INGREDIENTS:

- 1-pound ground duck
- 2 tablespoons Shaoxing cooking wine
- Zest and juice from 1 orange
- 1 tablespoon chopped fresh ginger
- 3 garlic cloves, crushed and chopped
- 1 tablespoon soy sauce
- 1 tablespoon Chinese five-spice powder
- 1 teaspoon spicy sesame oil
- ½ cup panko bread crumbs, divided
- Oil for deep-frying
- 2 tablespoons orange marmalade
- 2 tablespoons hoisin sauce
- ¼ cup ketchup

INSTRUCTIONS:

1. Combine the duck, wine, orange zest and juice, ginger, garlic, soy sauce, five-spice powder, sesame oil, and ¼ cup panko bread crumbs in a medium bowl. Mix well with chopsticks (but do not mash the mixture).

2. Make between 12 and 16 meatballs that are 1.5 inches wide. Use the last 1/4 cup of panko bread crumbs to cover each one.
3. About an inch of oil should be heated over high heat in the wok until the end of a wooden chopstick shows bubbles when dipped into the oil. For 3 minutes, fry the meatballs. Flip them over and cook for two or three minutes until golden brown. If you need more oil, add enough to cover half of the meatballs.
4. Make a glaze or dip for the meatballs by mixing the marmalade, hoisin sauce, and ketchup in a small bowl.

WOK-FRIED DUCK BREASTS AND HOISIN SAUCE WITH BOK CHOY

The wok's small space is great for keeping the duck's juices and flavour while letting the fat drain away. The trick is to heat the duck breast at just the right temperature to melt the fat so you can stir-fry the veggies without cooking the duck too much.

INGREDIENTS:
- 4 (4-ounce) boneless, skin-on duck breasts
- 2 tablespoons soy sauce
- 2 tablespoons Shaoxing cooking wine
- 1 tablespoon toasted sesame oil
- 1 teaspoon cornstarch
- 1 tablespoon chopped fresh ginger
- 3 garlic cloves, crushed and chopped
- 1 medium red onion, cut into ½-inch pieces
- 2 cups bok choy, sliced into ½-inch pieces
- 2 tablespoons hoisin sauce

- 4 scallions, both white and green parts, sliced into ¼-inch pieces
- Rice or noodles for serving
- Lightly score the skin of the duck breasts with perpendicular cuts ¼ inch apart.

INSTRUCTIONS:

1. Mix the duck breasts, soy sauce, wine, sesame oil, cornstarch, and corn in a big bowl or a bag with a zip-top. (Rubbing them in a plastic bag is a great way to do this.)
2. Over medium-high heat, put the duck breasts in the pan with the skin side down. Cook for about two minutes or until the juices start to pop. Once the breasts start to pop, cook them for another 3 minutes or until the skin is light brown.
3. Turn the breasts over and let them cook for another minute. Then, cut them from the pot across the grain into 14-inch pieces.
4. Only 2 tablespoons of fat should be left in the wok. Amp up the heat.
5. Stir-fry the ginger, garlic, and onion for 1 minute or until they smell good.
6. In a stir-fry, cook the bok choy for 1 minute.
7. Bring the sliced duck back to the wok and stir-fry it for 1 minute or until everything is well mixed.
8. Stir-fry the hoisin sauce and onions for 1 minute or until everything is well combined. Serve over noodles or rice.

HAWAIIAN HULI HULI SMOKED-CHICKEN STIR-FRY

This Hawaiian food, whose name means "turn" or "flip," is great for stir-frying. The fact that the pineapple tastes like it was smoked shows that the dish came from a tropical barbecue. A piece of aluminium foil, a rack, and a pan cover is needed for this recipe.

INGREDIENTS:

- 2 tablespoons loose Earl Grey tea
- ¼ cup brown sugar
- ¼ cup uncooked long-grain white rice
- 2 tablespoons all-purpose flour
- 1 pound boneless, skinless chicken thighs (2 or 3 thighs)
- 2 or 3 rings of canned pineapple (1 for each thigh)
- 2 tablespoons light soy sauce
- 2 tablespoons Shaoxing cooking wine
- 1 tablespoon cornstarch
- 2 tablespoons cooking oil
- 1 tablespoon chopped fresh ginger
- 3 garlic cloves, crushed and chopped
- 4 scallions, both white and green parts, cut into ¼-inch pieces of Rice for serving

INSTRUCTIONS:

1. Mix the tea leaves, brown sugar, rice, and flour on a square piece of aluminium foil, then roll up the sides to make a shallow saucer that is about 12 inches deep. It should have an open top. Put the paper plate in the wok's bottom.

2. Put a rack and a shelf with the chicken legs in the wok. Put a pineapple ring on each leg. Use a lid with a cap to cover the wok.

3. If you're cooking inside, open any windows near the stove and turn up the speed of your vent fan. If you can't get the air out of the room, do the following steps outside.

4. Turn up the heat. As the mix heats up, smoke will come out of it. At first, the smoke will be white. Then, it will be a light yellow colour and a darker yellow colour. When it turns dark yellow, which should take about 5 minutes, turn the heat down and set a timer for 10 minutes. Cook for 3 minutes for a light smoke. Cook for 5 to 10 minutes longer to make the smoke stronger.

5. Take the smoked chicken out and cut it across the grain into 14-inch pieces. Mix well when you add the soy sauce, wine, and cornstarch. Cut the pineapple rings into eight pieces and put them aside. Throw away the burning mixture and the foil.

6. Heat the oil in the pot over medium-high heat until it shines.

7. Stir-fry the ginger, garlic, smoked chicken, and any liquid for about two minutes or until the food smells good.

8. Stir-fry the smoked pineapple for one minute to mix it well.

9. Stir-fry the onions for one minute to make sure they are well combined. in addition to the rice.

SPICY HONEY SESAME CHICKEN AND BROCCOLI STIR-FRY

This easy stir-fry is a great example of how velveting can add flavour and smooth food. The crunchy veggies and spicy-sweet sauce go well with steamed rice or noodles.

INGREDIENTS:

- 1 pound boneless, skinless chicken thighs, sliced into ¼-inch pieces across the grain
- 1 teaspoon spicy sesame oil
- 2 tablespoons Shaoxing cooking wine
- 2 tablespoons light soy sauce
- 1 tablespoon cornstarch
- 2 tablespoons cooking oil
- 1 tablespoon chopped fresh ginger
- 3 garlic cloves, crushed and chopped
- 2 cups broccoli florets ¼ cup honey
- 4 scallions, both white and green parts, cut into ¼-inch pieces for garnishing
- 1 tablespoon toasted sesame seeds for garnishing
- Rice or noodles for serving

INSTRUCTIONS:

1. Combine the chicken thighs, sesame oil, wine, soy sauce, and cornstarch in a big bowl.
2. Over medium-high heat, heat the oil in the wok until it shines. Add the chicken legs, ginger, and garlic, but save the liquid. Stir-fry the food for two minutes or until it browns and smells good.
3. Stir-fry the broccoli for one minute or until it turns bright green.

4. Stir-fry for 1 minute or until the broccoli is crisp-tender and the chicken is done. Add the honey and the rest of the juice from the chicken.
5. Add the onions and sesame seeds on top. Serve over noodles or rice.

TERIYAKI CHICKEN MEATBALLS

"Teri" in Japanese means "shine" or "glaze," and "yaki" means "grill" or "roast." These sweet and salty chicken meatballs have a lot of umami and are great as a starter, on top of rice or noodles, or as a snack for a party.

INGREDIENTS:
- 1 pound ground chicken
- 2 tablespoons Shaoxing cooking wine
- 2 tablespoons dark soy sauce
- 2 tablespoons honey
- 1 tablespoon chopped fresh ginger
- 3 garlic cloves, crushed and chopped
- 1 teaspoon toasted sesame oil
- ½ cup panko bread crumbs, divided
- Oil for frying
- 2 tablespoons light soy sauce
- 2 tablespoons rice vinegar
- 1 tablespoon miso paste

INSTRUCTIONS:
1. Mix the chicken, wine, dark soy sauce, honey, ginger, garlic, sesame oil, and 1/4 cup of panko bread crumbs in a medium bowl.

2. Make 12 to 16 1.5-inch meatballs and roll them lightly in the last 1/4 cup of panko bread crumbs.
3. Heat about an inch of oil in the wok over medium-high heat until it hits 350°F or until you can make bubbles in the oil with the tip of a wooden chopstick. In a pan, cook the meatballs for 4 minutes. Fry them for another 3 or 4 minutes until they are golden brown.
4. Mix the light soy sauce, vinegar, and miso in a small bowl and use it as a dip for the meatballs.

ORANGE CHICKEN

Orange chicken is a dish from the province of Hunan that has become famous because of the fast-food chain Panda Express. Instead of deep-frying the chicken, we stir-fry it to keep things healthy. Fresh orange peel is the most important thing. It gives the sauce a sweet and sour taste.

INGREDIENTS:
- For the marinade
- 2 (5-ounce) boneless chicken breast halves cut into bite-size pieces
- 3 teaspoons cornstarch
- 2 teaspoons soy sauce
- 2 pinches of ground white pepper
- For the sauce, 3 or 4 orange peel strips, julienned
- 2 tablespoons water
- 2 tablespoons apple cider vinegar
- 1 tablespoon orange juice
- 2 teaspoons brown sugar
- 2 teaspoons cornstarch
- 1 teaspoon soy sauce

- ½ teaspoon ketchup
- 2-star anise petals
- 1 clove Pinch of red pepper flakes
- For the stir-fry
- 2 tablespoons peanut oil
- 1 scallion, both white and green parts, chopped for garnishing
- ½ teaspoon toasted sesame seeds for garnishing
- To make the marinade

INSTRUCTIONS:

1. Toss the chicken with cornstarch, soy sauce, and white pepper. Let sit at room temperature for 20 minutes. To make the sauce,
2. Mix the orange peel, water, apple cider vinegar, orange juice, brown sugar, cornstarch, soy sauce, ketchup, cloves, star anise, and red pepper flakes in a small bowl. Set it aside. How to make stir-fried food Heat the peanut oil in a pot over medium-high heat.
3. In a stir-fry, cook the chicken until it turns a light brown. Other than the pan, put the chicken somewhere else.
4. The sauce will get thicker as you stir it in the wok.
5. Bring the chicken back to the pan and stir it so that each piece is covered.
6. Put it on a plate and sprinkle it with the onions and sesame seeds. Serve right away.

INDONESIAN FRIED DUCK-BREAST BITES

The outside of these duck nuggets is crunchy, but the inside is juicy and soft. They make a great starter or small plate wrapped in lettuce and dipped in homemade sriracha.

INGREDIENTS:

- 1 pound boneless, skin-on duck breast, cut into quarters
- 2 tablespoons dark soy sauce or keep
- manis (Indonesian sweet soy sauce)
- 1 teaspoon fish sauce
- 1 teaspoon spicy sesame oil
- 4 to 8 lettuce leaves
- Sriracha sauce for dipping

INSTRUCTIONS:

1. Make cuts in the duck skin that are 14 inches apart and cross each other.
2. Put the duck parts in the wok with the skin side down. Turn the heat to medium-high and wait about 2 minutes until they sizzle. Cook for about 4 or 5 minutes or until the skin goes golden.
3. To make the breast quarters medium-rare, flip them over and let them cook for 2 minutes.
4. Take the breasts out of the pot, pour off the duck fat, and cut them against the grain into pieces that are 12 inches long.
5. Slice the duck and add it to the pan with dark soy sauce, fish sauce, and sesame oil. Stir-fry on medium for one

minute or until the duck is medium-rare. Serve with Sriracha sauce covered in lettuce leaves.

PEKING DUCK STIR-FRY (FAN CHAO YA)

This standard stir-fry is great with duck breasts instead of chicken because duck breasts are meaty and have a lot of flavours. Duck can handle the stronger tastes in dark, rich Peking-style sauces better than chicken, which goes well with lighter Cantonese sauces.

INGREDIENTS:

- 2 tablespoons light soy sauce
- 1 tablespoon Shaoxing cooking wine
- 1 tablespoon sugar
- 1 tablespoon toasted sesame oil
- 1 tablespoon cornstarch
- 1 pound boneless, skinless duck breasts, cut into ¼-inch pieces across the grain
- 2 tablespoons cooking oil
- 3 garlic cloves, crushed and chopped
- 1 tablespoon chopped fresh ginger
- 4 scallions, both white and green parts, sliced into ¼-inch pieces
- ¼ cup hoisin sauce
- Rice or noodles for serving

INSTRUCTIONS:

1. In a medium bowl, mix the duck slices with the soy sauce, wine, sugar, sesame oil, cornstarch, and cornstarch.

2. Over medium-high heat, heat the oil in the wok until it shines.
3. Stir-fry the duck with the garlic, ginger, and any sauce left in the bowl for 2 minutes or until the duck is lightly browned.
4. Stir-fry the onions, hoisin sauce, and the sauce you saved for 1 minute or until everything is well combined.
5. Serve over noodles or rice.

TEA-SMOKED DUCK BREAST (ZHANGCHA YA)

This is a great way to split the duck breasts and smoke them using your wok. You will need a lid that fits pretty well, a wok rack, and aluminium foil to smoke. If you do this inside, you will also need an air fan and windows that can be opened. Because of this, I usually cook this and other smoked foods outside.

INGREDIENTS:
- 4 boneless, skin-on duck breasts
- 1 teaspoon of acceptable sea salt
- 2 tablespoons loose jasmine tea
- ¼ cup uncooked long-grain white rice
- ¼ cup brown sugar
- 2 tablespoons all-purpose flour
- Plum sauce for dipping

INSTRUCTIONS:
1. Cut 1/4-inch-wide slits in the duck skin that cross each other. Don't cut into the meat by mistake.
2. Put the breasts in the wok with the skin side down. Heat the wok on medium-high until the fat sizzles and

separates. Then turn the heat down to medium and cook for 5 minutes more.

3. Get rid of the fat in the wok. Turn the duck breast over and cook for 5 minutes more.

4. Take the duck breasts out of the wok, drain the fat, and wash the pan.

5. Mix the tea leaves, rice, brown sugar, and flour on a square piece of aluminium foil, and then roll up the sides to make a shallow saucer that is about 12 inches deep. It should have an open top. Put the paper plate in the wok's bottom.

6. Stack the duck breasts on a shelf inside the wok. Use a lid with a cap to cover the wok.

7. If you're cooking inside, open any windows near the stove and turn up the speed of your vent fan. If you can't get the air out of the room, do the following steps outside.

8. Turn up the heat. As the mix heats up, smoke will come out of it. At first, the smoke will be white. Then, it will be a light yellow colour and a darker yellow colour. After about 5 minutes, when it turns dark yellow, turn the heat down to low.

9. Set a timer for 3 minutes for a light smoke. If you want the smoke to strengthen, smoke the breasts for 5–10 minutes longer. Take off the breasts and cut them across the grain into pieces that are 12 inches long. The plum sauce can be added to the dish.

FIVE-SPICE CHICKEN AND CUCUMBER STIR-FRY (WUXIANG FEN GAI)

Soft, moist chicken legs go well with fresh, crunchy cucumbers. We don't remove the skins because they add colour, taste, and fibre to the food. This is ready in 20 minutes or less for bowls of steamed rice.

INGREDIENTS:

- 1 pound boneless, skinless chicken thighs sliced into
- ¼-inch strips against the grain
- 1 tablespoon Chinese five-spice powder
- 2 tablespoons Shaoxing cooking wine
- 2 tablespoons light soy sauce
- 1 tablespoon brown sugar
- 1 teaspoon spicy sesame oil
- 1 tablespoon cornstarch
- 2 tablespoons cooking oil
- 1 tablespoon chopped fresh ginger
- 2 garlic cloves, crushed and chopped
- 2 cups cucumbers, skin on (run a fork along their
- lengths to break up the skin before slicing them into bite-size pieces)
- 4 scallions, both white and green parts, cut into ¼-inch pieces of Rice or noodles for serving

INSTRUCTIONS:

1. Mix the chicken, five-spice powder, wine, soy sauce, brown sugar, sesame oil, and cornstarch in a medium bowl.

2. Over medium-high heat, heat the oil in the wok until it shines.
3. Add the chicken, ginger, and garlic, but save the juice. Stir-fry for 2 minutes, until fragrant.
4. Add the cucumber slices and the rest of the juice. Stir-fry for 1 minute or until the chicken and veggies are warm.
5. Stir-fry the onions for one minute to ensure they are well mixed in. Serve over noodles or rice.

STEAMED CHICKEN, CABBAGE, AND CHINESE SAUSAGE (LAP CHEONG GAI)

This easy-to-make Chinese steamed meatloaf pie is delicious and simple to make. The Chinese sausage (lap Cheong) is a dry, cured, and sweet sausage you can buy at Asian stores and online.

INGREDIENTS:
- 8 ounces ground chicken
- 4 ounces lap Cheong Chinese sausage (2 or 3 links), finely chopped
- 2 cups chopped
- Chinese cabbage (or bok choy, napa, or American cabbage)
- 3 large eggs, scrambled
- 3 tablespoons light soy sauce
- 2 tablespoons
- Shaoxing cooking wine
- Rice or noodles for serving

INSTRUCTIONS:

1. Cut up the chicken, sausage, broccoli, eggs, soy sauce, and wine in a food processor until they are all the same size. Spread the mixture in a pie pan or a small dish.
2. Bring two inches of water to a boil in the pan over high heat. Put a rack and a shelf in the wok. Cover and steam for 15 minutes. If you need to, add more water to ensure the food is cooked all through.
3. Serve over noodles or rice.

SWEET-AND-SOUR CHICKEN (GU LAO JI)

This is a standard Cantonese stir-fry, but it doesn't have a thick batter or a sweet sauce. The onions and red peppers add more taste, and you can add pineapple if you want, but you don't have to.

INGREDIENTS:

- 1 pound boneless, skinless chicken thighs, cut into ¼-inch pieces across the grain
- 2 tablespoons brown sugar
- 2 tablespoons Shaoxing cooking wine
- 2 tablespoons rice vinegar
- 1 tablespoon light soy sauce
- ¼ cup ketchup
- 2 tablespoons cooking oil
- 1 tablespoon chopped fresh ginger
- 2 garlic cloves, crushed and chopped
- 1 medium onion, cut into ½-inch pieces
- 1 medium red bell pepper, cut into ½-inch pieces
- 1 teaspoon cornstarch

- 4 scallions, both white and green parts, cut into ¼-inch pieces
- Rice or noodles for serving

INSTRUCTIONS:

1. Mix the chicken strips, brown sugar, wine, vinegar, soy sauce, and ketchup in a bowl.
2. Heat the oil in the pot over medium-high heat until it shines. Add the ginger, garlic, and chicken, keeping any liquid, and stir-fry for two minutes or until the chicken smells good.
3. Stir-fry the onion for 1 minute. Stir-fry the bell pepper for one minute or until the onion falls apart.
4. Add the cornstarch and the juice you saved to the wok and stir-fry for about 2 minutes until a glaze forms and the chicken is done.
5. Add the onions and serve with rice or noodles.

GARLIC CHICKEN (SUAN JI)

Besides cooked rice, this might be the easiest thing to make. You only need five things, not counting the oil, and the rice will be ready in about 15 minutes. You can add your favourite herbs and spices to the recipe to make it more interesting, but sometimes easy is best.

INGREDIENTS:

- 1 pound boneless, skinless chicken thighs, cut into ¼-inch pieces across the grain
- 2 tablespoons dark soy sauce
- 2 tablespoons cooking oil
- 1 tablespoon chopped fresh ginger

- 4 garlic cloves, crushed and chopped
- 4 scallions, both white and green parts, cut into ¼-inch pieces
- Rice or noodles for serving

INSTRUCTIONS:

1. In a medium bowl, mix the chicken and dark soy sauce.
2. Over medium-high heat, heat the oil in the wok until it shines.
3. Add the chicken, ginger, and garlic, and stir-fry for 3 minutes until the chicken is cooked and smells good.
4. For one minute, stir-fry the onions to mix them in. Serve over rice or noodles.

GRACE TOY'S FRIED CHICKEN

We finally figured out how to make my mom's famous fried chicken with the help of my sister Kathi and my cousin Linda. This is how the dish we grew up with tastes when stir-fried. Note: Depending on how many people you're cooking for and how big your pot is, you may need to cook this in batches.

INGREDIENTS:

- 1 cup pancake baking mix (such as Bisquick)
- 1 teaspoon garlic salt
- ½ teaspoon freshly ground black pepper
- 1 pound boneless, skinless chicken thighs cut into 1-inch squares (nuggets)
- Cooking oil for shallow frying
- Rice and vegetables for serving

INSTRUCTIONS:

1. Mix the pancake, garlic, salt, and pepper in a medium bowl.
2. Put the dry mixture on the chicken, wait 5 minutes, and then put it on again.
3. Heat enough oil to cover about half of the chicken pieces in the pot. Remember that the oil level will rise as you add more chicken. Heat the oil to 350 F or until a chopstick tip dipped in it makes bubbles around it.
4. Put the chicken in the oil and fry it for three or four minutes or until the covering is golden brown. Flip it over and cook for another 3 or 4 minutes.
5. After taking the food out of the pan, dry it on paper towels. Serve with rice and a side of veggies.

THAI PEANUT CHICKEN LETTUCE WRAPS

Spicy stir-fried chicken is wrapped in sweet, crunchy lettuce leaves and topped with bean sprouts, parsley, peanuts, and lime. Why wouldn't you like it? Don't forget to add a sweet and hot peanut sriracha sauce at the end.

INGREDIENTS:

- 1 pound boneless, skinless chicken thighs, cut into ¼-inch pieces against the grain
- 1 teaspoon fish sauce
- 1 teaspoon sesame oil
- Zest and juice of
- 1 lime
- tablespoon brown sugar
- 1 tablespoon cornstarch

- 2 tablespoons cooking oil
- ½ cup chopped peanuts
- 1 tablespoon honey
- 2 cups bean sprouts, rinsed and drained
- ½ cup chopped fresh cilantro
- ¼ cup peanut butter
- 1 cup sriracha sauce
- 8 lettuce leaves
- 4 lime wedges for serving

INSTRUCTIONS:

1. In a medium bowl, combine the chicken with the fish sauce, sesame oil, lime juice and zest, brown sugar, and cornstarch.
2. Over medium-high heat, heat the oil in the wok until it shines. Add the chicken, save the juice, and stir-fry for 2 minutes, until the chicken is cooked.
3. Stir fry the peanuts, honey, and the rest of the juice for two minutes or until a glaze forms.
4. Remove the pan from the heat and add the bean sprouts and parsley.
5. Mix the peanut butter and sriracha sauce in a small bowl to make a dip.
6. Wrap the chicken in lettuce leaves, squeeze lime juice, dip it in the sauce, and eat.

GREEN TEA–SMOKED LEMON CHICKEN

This is done in two steps. First, boneless chicken legs are slowly smoked in the wok. After the chicken is cut into thin pieces and smoothed out, it is quickly stir-fried with scallions. You will need a piece of metal foil, a rack, and a wok cover to smoke the chicken.

INGREDIENTS:

- ¼ cup uncooked long-grain white rice
- ¼ cup green tea leaves
- 2 tablespoons all-purpose flour
- 2 tablespoons brown sugar
- Coarsely chopped zest and juice of
- 1 lemon
- 1 pound boneless, skinless chicken thighs (3 or 4 thighs)
- 2 tablespoons light soy sauce
- 2 tablespoons
- Shaoxing cooking wine
- 1 tablespoon cornstarch
- 2 tablespoons cooking oil
- 1 tablespoon chopped fresh ginger
- 2 garlic cloves, crushed and chopped
- 4 scallions, both white and green parts, cut into
- ¼-inch pieces
- Rice or noodles for serving

INSTRUCTIONS:

1. Mix the rice, tea leaves, flour, brown sugar, and lemon zest on a square piece of aluminium foil. Roll up the sides

to make a shallow, 12-inch-deep saucer. It should have an open top. Put the paper plate in the wok's bottom.

2. Put a rack in the wok and the chicken legs on the rack above the mixture. Use a dome-shaped lid to cover.

3. Open the windows near the stove and turn the vent fan high if cooking inside. If you can't get the air outside, you must do the following.

4. Turn up the heat until smoke starts to come out of the mixture. At first, the smoke will be white. Then, it will be a light yellow colour and a darker yellow colour. When it turns dark yellow, which should take about 5 minutes, turn down the heat and start counting.

5. Set a timer for 3 minutes for a light smoke. If you want a stronger smoke, add 5 to 10 more minutes. Put out the fire and wait a minute.

6. Take out the chicken and cut it across the grain into 14-inch pieces.

7. Mix the sliced smoked chicken, lemon juice, soy sauce, wine, and cornstarch in a medium bowl.

8. Heat the oil in the pot over medium-high heat until it shines. Add the chicken, ginger, and garlic, but keep any liquid. Stir-fry the chicken for two minutes or until it has a nice colour and smell.

9. Add the juice you saved and stir-fry for another minute until the chicken is done and a glaze forms.

10. Stir-fry the onions for one minute to mix them in. Serve over noodles or rice.

KUNG PAO SHRIMP

This seafood version of the famous Chinese-American dish has shrimp, bell pepper, and roasted peanuts in a tasty sauce that can be a little (or a lot) spicy. It looks, feels, and tastes great and is ready in just 15 minutes. It goes well with meals with more than one course.

INGREDIENTS:

For the sauce
- 2 tablespoons rice vinegar
- 2 tablespoons light soy sauce
- 2 teaspoons brown sugar
- 1 teaspoon dark soy sauce
- 1 teaspoon sesame oil
- 1 teaspoon cornstarch

For the stir-fry
- 2 tablespoons cooking oil
- 8 to 10 dried red chiles
- 1 small green bell pepper (or ½ a large one), cut into bite-size pieces
- 2-inch piece ginger, julienned
- 2 garlic cloves, crushed and chopped
- 1 pound shrimp, peeled and deveined
- ¼ cup unsalted roasted peanuts
- 1 or 2 scallions, both white and green parts, cut into 1-inch pieces of Steamed rice for serving

To make the sauce

INSTRUCTIONS:

1. Mix the rice vinegar, the light soy sauce, the brown sugar, the dark soy sauce, the sesame oil, and the cornstarch in a small bowl. Mix well, then put to the side. How to make stir-fried food
2. Heat the oil in the pot over medium heat until it sparkles.
3. Stir-fry the chiles and bell pepper for 3 minutes or until the skin of the bell pepper starts to bubble.
4. Stir-fry the ginger and garlic for about 20 seconds or until they smell good.
5. Spread the shrimp out in a single line on the pan. The shrimp are cooked on the bottom, turned over, and stir-fried for about a minute or until finished.
6. Add the peanuts and sauce and stir.
7. When the sauce gets thick, turn off the heat and add the onions. Put into a serving dish and serve with rice that has been steamed.

STEAMED GINGER, GARLIC, AND SCALLION SALMON

In a small bowl, stir together the rice vinegar, light soy sauce, brown sugar, dark soy sauce, sesame oil, and cornstarch. Mix well, and then put it to the side. How to make stir-fry Heat the oil in the pot over medium heat until it shimmers.Stir-fry the chiles and bell pepper for 3 minutes or until the skin on the bell pepper starts to brown. Stir-fry the ginger and garlic for about 20 seconds until they smell good.

Spread the shrimp in a single line and put them in the pan. After cooking on the bottom, the shrimp are turned over and stir-fried for about a minute or until finished.

Add the peanuts and the sauce and stir.

When the sauce gets thick, take it off the heat and add the onions. Put in a serving dish and serve with rice that has been warmed.

INGREDIENTS:

- 1½ pounds fresh salmon fillet
- 2 tablespoons chopped fresh ginger
- 4 garlic cloves, crushed and chopped
- 4 scallions, both white and green parts, minced
- ¼ cup dark soy sauce
- 1 tablespoon Shaoxing cooking wine
- Rice, for serving

INSTRUCTIONS:

1. Cut the salmon fillet into four pieces and put them in a pie pan or another small dish.

2. About halfway through the fillets, make two cuts perpendicular to each other and an inch apart. Mix ginger, garlic, onions, soy sauce, and wine in a small bowl to make a rough pesto.
3. Spread the pesto on the fish and push it into the cuts.
4. Bring an inch of water to a boil in the pan over high heat. Add a rack to the wok and a shelf to the top of the pan. For medium-rare, cover the fish and steam it for 5 minutes per inch of thickness. Picking it with a fork or chopstick will make it clear and thin.
5. Mix in with the rice.

HONEY WALNUT SHRIMP

From Hong Kong comes this tasty dish with fish. It is based on the Cantonese flavours of ginger, garlic, and scallions, and people worldwide now eat it at home and in places.

INGREDIENTS:
- 1 cup water
- 1 cup sugar
- 1 cup walnuts
- 1 large egg
- ¼ cup cornstarch
- 1 teaspoon kosher salt
- ½ teaspoon ground white pepper
- 1 pound medium shrimp, peeled and deveined
- ¼ cup vegetable oil
- 2 tablespoons crushed and chopped fresh ginger
- 3 garlic cloves, crushed and chopped
- 1 medium onion, diced into

- ½-inch pieces
- 1 red bell pepper, diced into
- ½-inch pieces
- 1 bunch (6 to 8) scallions, cut into
- ½-inch pieces
- ¼ cup honey
- ¼ cup mayonnaise
- 2 tablespoons rice wine
- 2 tablespoons soy sauce
- Steamed rice for serving
- Chopped cilantro for serving (optional)

INSTRUCTIONS:

1. Heat the water and sugar in a small pan over medium-high heat until the water boils and the sugar is dissolved.
2. Add the walnuts to the boiling water and let it boil for a minute. Move the nuts to a plate lined with paper towels so they can drain.
3. In a small bowl, beat the egg. Mix the cornstarch, salt, and white pepper in another small bowl.
4. Dip each shrimp in the egg, then roll it around in the cornstarch mixture to coat it evenly.
5. Heat the oil on high in a wok or big cast-iron pan until it sparkles. Stir-fry the shrimp until golden brown, which should take about 3 minutes. Place the fried shrimp on a plate.
6. All but 2 tablespoons of the oil in the pan should be taken out and thrown away. Stir-fry the ginger and garlic for about a minute until they turn brown.
7. Stir-fry the onion for 1 minute. Stir-fry the bell pepper for 1 minute. Stir-fry for 1 minute after adding the onions.
8. Mix the honey, mayonnaise, rice wine, and soy sauce in a small bowl. Pour the sauce into the pot and stir-fry for

about two minutes or until a glaze forms. Add the shrimp and walnuts and mix to coat.

9. Add to cooked rice. If you want, you can top the dish with mint.

SHRIMP WITH LOBSTER SAUCE

When people order this food for the first time, they are often confused because there is no lobster in the sauce. Instead, it has big, juicy shrimp in a thick sauce with egg, carrots, and green peas. It's great once you overcome the fact that there's no lobster. Serve it with heated white or brown rice to soak up all the sauce in a multi-course meal.

INGREDIENTS:

For the sauce
- 1 cup chicken broth
- 2 teaspoons light soy sauce
- 2 teaspoons cornstarch
- 1 teaspoon
- Shaoxing cooking wine
- ½ teaspoon sugar
- Pinch ground white pepper
- For the stir-fry
- 1 tablespoon cooking oil
- 2-inch piece ginger, julienned
- 2 garlic cloves, minced
- ½ cup frozen peas and carrots
- 1 pound large shrimp, peeled and deveined
- 1 large egg, lightly beaten

To make the sauce

INSTRUCTIONS:

1. Mix the chicken broth, soy sauce, cornstarch, wine, sugar, and white pepper in a small bowl. Mix everything well and break up any lumps that form. Set aside. How to make a stir-fry

2. Heat the oil in the pot over medium-high heat until it shines.

3. Stir-fry the ginger and garlic for about 20 seconds or until the food smells good.

4. Stir-fry the frozen peas and carrots for 10 seconds to mix them in.

5. Shrimp and sauce should be added to the pan. Mix all of the ingredients with a wok spoon.

6. Slowly pour in the beaten egg while stirring with the wok's spoon. When the shrimp are done cooking and curled into a "C" shape, put the dish on a serving plate and serve it immediately.

DRUNKEN SHRIMP

This recipe shows how creative Chinese cooking can be by using the liquid to prepare the meat as the finishing liquid. The key is not letting the shrimp rest for more than 30 minutes. Shrimp are so delicate that they can get tough if they sit in the sauce for too long. The goji berries give this dish a sweet and sour taste, but you don't have to use them. Instead, you can use very small pieces of dried cherries.

INGREDIENTS:

- 2 cups Shaoxing cooking wine
- 4 peeled fresh ginger slices, each about the size of a quarter
- 2 tablespoons dried goji berries (optional)
- 2 teaspoons sugar
- 1 pound jumbo shrimp, peeled and deveined, tails left on
- 2 tablespoons cooking oil
- Kosher salt
- 2 teaspoons cornstarch

INSTRUCTIONS:

1. Mix the wine, ginger, (if using) goji berries, and sugar in a large bowl until the sugar is dissolved. Add shrimp and put the lid on. Let the flavours mix in the refrigerator for 20 to 30 minutes.
2. Pour the shrimp and marinade into a colander set over a bowl. Keep 1/2 cup of the marinade and throw out the rest.
3. Over medium-high heat, heat the oil in the wok until it shines. Put a little salt in the oil and stir it around.

4. Stir-fry the shrimp quickly, flipping and tossing them in the wok as you add a pinch of salt. Keep moving the shrimp around for about 3 minutes until they turn pink.
5. Mix the reserved marinade with the cornstarch and pour it over the shrimp. Toss the shrimp with the marinade. It will thicken into a shiny sauce as soon as it boils. About 5 minutes more will be needed.
6. Throw away the ginger and put the shrimp and goji berries on a plate. Prepare hot.

WHOLE STEAMED FISH WITH SIZZLING GINGER AND SCALLIONS (HONG ZHENG YU)

Whole sea bass, red snapper, yellowtail snapper, rockfish, trout, or halibut are my favourite fish to cook. This is also a great way to cook a whole fish, which we've done many times. When you buy a whole fish at the market, ask the butcher to clean it so it's ready to cook as soon as you get home. Add thin slices of fresh peppers to give the sauce a little heat. For the fish.

INGREDIENTS:
- 1 whole whitefish, about
- 2 pounds, head-on and cleaned
- ½ cup kosher salt for cleaning
- 3 scallions, both white and green parts, sliced into
- 3-inch pieces
- 4 peeled, fresh ginger slices, each about the size of a quarter

- 2 tablespoons
- Shaoxing cooking wine For the sauce
- 2 tablespoons light soy sauce
- 1 tablespoon sesame oil
- 2 teaspoons sugar
- For the sizzling ginger oil
- 3 tablespoons cooking oil
- 2 tablespoons peeled fresh ginger, finely julienned into thin strips, divided
- 2 scallions, both white and green parts, thinly sliced, divided
- Red onion, thinly sliced (optional)
- Chopped fresh cilantro (optional)

To make the fish

INSTRUCTIONS:

1. Use kosher salt to salt the fish all over, inside and out. Rinse the fish, and then pat it dry with a paper towel.
2. Put half of the onions and ginger on a big plate that will fit into a bamboo steamer basket. Place the fish on top and stuff it with the left ginger and onions. Fish and wine should be mixed.
3. Run cold water over a bamboo steamer pan and lid, then put them in the wok. Pour about 2 inches of cold water into the steamer so that the water is about 1/4 to 1/2 inch above the bottom of the steamer but not so high that it hits the bottom of the basket. Get the water boiling.
4. Cover the plate and put it in the steamer basket. Steam the fish for 15 minutes over medium heat. For every half-pound more, add 2 minutes. Use a fork to poke the fish near the head before you take it out of the pan. When the meat falls apart, it's done. If the heart is stuck together,

give it two more minutes of steaming. While the fish is cooking, put the soy sauce, sesame oil, and sugar in a small pan and heat them on low. Set aside.

5. Put the fish on a clean plate when it's done. The cooking liquid and aromatics on the steamed plate should be thrown away. Before the fish gets cold. Cover it with aluminium foil to keep it warm while you prepare the oil. To make oil that crackles,

6. In a small pot over medium heat, heat the cooking oil. Add half of the ginger and onions and cook for 10 seconds before it smokes. Put the fish in the oil that is already very hot.

7. Add the rest of the ginger, scallions, red onion (if you're using it), and cilantro (if you're using it), and serve immediately.

SMOKED-TEA TILAPIA

Tilapia is one of the fish that can be grown the most safely. If you want to buy fish, I suggest it because it is usually fresh and hasn't been frozen. The mild taste and light smell of the smoked tea go well together. You can easily smoke fish in a wok with a rack, metal foil, and a lid.

INGREDIENTS:

- 1 pound fresh tilapia fillets (3 or 4 fillets)
- 2 tablespoons Shaoxing cooking wine
- 2 tablespoons light soy sauce
- 1 tablespoon toasted sesame oil
- ¼ cup uncooked long-grain white rice
- ¼ cup loose black oolong tea
- 2 tablespoons brown sugar

- Rice, for serving Vegetables, for serving

INSTRUCTIONS:

1. Put the fish, wine, soy sauce, and sesame oil in a bag with a zipper and rub it all over to cover.

2. Mix the rice, tea leaves, and brown sugar on a square piece of aluminium foil, and then roll up the sides to make a shallow saucer that is about 12 inches deep. It should have an open top. Put the paper plate in the wok's bottom.

3. Put a rack in the wok and place the fish and other seasonings on top. Use a dome-shaped lid to cover.

4. If you're cooking inside, open any windows near the stove and turn up the speed of your vent fan. If you can't get the air out of the room, do the following steps outside.

5. Turn up the heat. As the mix heats up, smoke will come out of it. At first, the smoke will be white. Then, it will be a light yellow colour and a darker yellow colour. Turn down the heat when it turns dark yellow, which will take about 5 minutes.

6. Let the fish smoke for five minutes over low heat, then turn off the heat and wait five minutes before checking on it. It will be rough and a dark brown colour. Serve over rice with veggies on the side.

SHRIMP AND SQUID STIR-FRY WITH BOK CHOY

To stir-fry squid well, you only need two minutes or less. It gets hard after 2 minutes. I think it's done when the tentacles start to curl. If you cook it too long, you'll have to cook it for another hour to make it soft again. Shrimp and bok choy, which cook quickly in the wok, go well.

INGREDIENTS:

- 8 ounces large shrimp, shelled, deveined, and cut in half lengthwise
- 8 ounces of squid tentacles and rings
- 4 tablespoons
- Shaoxing cooking wine, divided
- 4 tablespoons light soy sauce, divided
- 2 tablespoons toasted sesame oil, divided
- 2 tablespoons cornstarch, divided
- 2 tablespoons cooking oil
- 1 tablespoon chopped fresh ginger
- 2 garlic cloves, crushed and chopped
- 1 (15-ounce) can of straw mushrooms, drained and rinsed
- 2 cups bok choy cut into
- ½-inch pieces
- 4 scallions, both white and green parts, cut into
- ¼-inch pieces
- Rice or noodles for serving

INSTRUCTIONS:

1. Mix half of the shrimp, squid, wine, soy sauce, sesame oil, and cornstarch in two medium bowls.

2. Over medium-high heat, heat the oil in the wok until it shines.
3. Add the shrimp, ginger, and garlic. Save any liquid and stir-fry for 2 minutes or until the shrimp smells good.
4. Stir-fry the shrimp and mushrooms for one minute or until the shrimp is clear.
5. Stir-fry the bok choy for one minute or until it turns a bright green colour.
6. Stir-fry the squid for one minute, saving any liquid, until it curls.
7. Stir-fry the rest of the liquids and the onions for 1 minute to make a light glaze. Serve over noodles or rice.

STEAMED SHRIMP AND SCALLOPS WITH STRAW MUSHROOMS IN OYSTER SAUCE

Shrimp and scallops that have been steamed and lightly covered with oyster sauce go well with the umami flavour of the mushrooms. When the steamed shrimp is curled and clear, the cooking is done.

INGREDIENTS:

- 8 ounces large shrimp, shelled, deveined, and cut in half lengthwise
- 8 ounces fresh sea scallops. sliced in half coin-wise
- 1 (15-ounce) can of straw mushrooms, drained and rinsed
- ¼ cup oyster sauce
- 4 ounces ground pork

- 4 scallions, both white and green parts, cut into
- ¼-inch pieces
- Rice or noodles for serving

INSTRUCTIONS:

1. Cut the shrimp, scallops, and mushrooms into small pieces and put them in a pie pan or a flat dish.
2. Make loose chunks of the ground pork and oyster sauce with chopsticks. Then, put the pork on top of the other ingredients in the pie pan.
3. Scallions should be put on everything.
4. Bring an inch of water to a boil in the pan over high heat. Put a rack in the wok and a shelf on top of the pie pan. Cover it and let it steam for 10 minutes or until it's done.
5. Serve over noodles or rice.

SMOKY TEA-STEAMED OYSTERS

This simple two-step method for cooking and steaming fresh oysters is a quick and easy way to open and eat oysters. If you've ever used a can to smoke oysters, you'll notice that this method makes them taste better and stay soft. You will need a metal foil sheet, rack, and wok cover to smoke.

INGREDIENTS:

- ¼ cup lapsang souchong tea leaves
- ¼ cup uncooked long-grain white rice
- 2 tablespoons chopped fresh ginger
- 4 garlic cloves, crushed and chopped
- 2 tablespoons brown sugar
- 12 to 14 oysters, scrubbed
- ½ cup water

- 2 tablespoons sriracha sauce
- 2 tablespoons oyster sauce

INSTRUCTIONS:

1. Mix the tea leaves, rice, ginger, garlic, and brown sugar on a square piece of aluminium foil. Make a shallow saucer about 12 inches deep by rolling up the ends. It should have an open top. Put the paper plate in the wok's bottom.
2. If you're cooking inside, open any windows near the stove and turn up the speed of your vent fan. If you can't get the air out of the room, do the following steps outside.
3. Turn up the heat.
4. While the wood and smoke mixture is getting hot, put the oysters on a rack so that the cupped sides are on the bottom and the flat sides are on top. When you put the frame in the pan, ensure it is at least 2 inches taller than the foil.
5. Use a lid with a cap to cover the wok. As the mix heats up, smoke will come out of it. At first, the smoke will be white. Then, it will be a light yellow colour and a darker yellow colour. Wait 4 more minutes after the smoke turns dark yellow, which should take about 5 minutes. Then, pour the water into the wok between the lid and the edge without removing the lid. Keep your distance from the steam.
6. Let the oysters cook for 3–4 minutes or until the shells have opened.
7. In a small bowl, mix the sriracha and oyster sauce. Serve this with your cooked and smoked oysters.

WOK-FRIED WHOLE FISH (ZHA YU)

This is the classic dish for banquets, such as those for the Lunar New Year. The head always faces the honoured guest or, if there are no guests, the person in charge of the house. By the way, it's lucky to eat the eyes of a fish.

INGREDIENTS:

- ½ teaspoon kosher salt
- 2 (1-pound) fresh redfish, such as tilapia or porgy; cleaned, scaled, tail and fins cut off
- ⅓ cup cooking oil
- 2 tablespoons chopped fresh ginger
- 2 tablespoons
- Shaoxing cooking wine
- 2 tablespoons light soy sauce
- 1 teaspoon sugar
- 1 teaspoon sesame oil
- 4 scallions, both white and green parts, cut into
- ¼-inch pieces
- Salt both sides of each fish and set it aside.

INSTRUCTIONS:

1. Over medium-high heat, heat the oil in the wok until it shines.
2. Stir-fry the ginger until it smells good and the oil coats the inside of the pan.
3. Put the two fish in the wok and fry them for 4 or 5 minutes until they come away from the pan and a light crust forms. Turning and tilting the wok helps move the oil around the heads and tails.
4. If you need to, shake the pan and use a spatula to move the fish around. If you need to, add more oil and turn the

fish over to cook for another 3 or 4 minutes or until the other side has a light crust.

5. While the fish is cooking, mix the wine, soy sauce, sugar, and sesame oil in a small bowl. Put this sauce around the edge of the pan.
6. Turn up the heat to keep the sauce at a low boil. Shake the wok to get the fish out, then add the onions.
7. Put the fish on plates to serve, and then do that.

SICHUAN BOILED CODFISH (SHUI ZHU YU)

"Fish boiled in water" is what this dish is called in Chinese. Imagine a strong, savoury, and hot fish stew. Use fresh fish pieces whenever you can. I always change my food to reflect what's fresh and in season at the market. In many Chinese markets, you can choose from live fish in tanks.

INGREDIENTS:
- 1 pound codfish fillet, cut into
- ½-inch strips
- 2 tablespoons Shaoxing cooking wine
- 2 tablespoons light soy sauce
- 1 tablespoon cornstarch
- ¼ cup cooking oil
- 1 tablespoon chopped fresh ginger
- 4 garlic cloves, crushed and chopped
- 1 teaspoon Chinese five-spice powder
- 1 teaspoon dried Sichuan peppercorns
- 1 tablespoon spicy sesame oil
- 4 cups chicken broth

- ½ ounce dried, sliced shiitake mushrooms
- 1 cup napa cabbage cut into
- 1-inch strips
- 4 scallions, both white and green parts, cut into ¼-inch pieces

INSTRUCTIONS:

1. Mix the sliced fish, wine, soy sauce, and cornstarch in a small dish.
2. Heat the oil in the pot over medium-high heat until it shines.
3. Stir-fry the ginger, garlic, five-spice powder, Sichuan peppercorns, and spicy sesame oil for 1 minute or until the food smells good.
4. Bring to a boil, then add the mushrooms and chicken broth. Cook for 5 minutes or until the mushrooms are soft.
5. Cut up the fish and put it, the napa cabbage, and the onions in the broth. Simmer for two minutes or until you can see through the fish. Serve right away in hot bowls.

MUSSELS IN BLACK BEAN SAUCE (DOU GU BANG LEI)

You get a unique salty sauce when you add black bean sauce to mussels. They can be served with steamed rice as an appetizer or as one of several plates. You'll love how simple and cheap it is to make this dish.

INGREDIENTS:

For the sauce
- 1 cup water
- 1 tablespoon black bean sauce
- 1 teaspoon rice vinegar
- 1 teaspoon sugar
- 1 teaspoon light soy sauce
- ½ teaspoon dark soy sauce

For the stir-fry
- 1 tablespoon cooking oil
- 2-inch piece ginger, peeled and julienned
- 2 garlic cloves, minced
- 2 pounds fresh mussels, scrubbed and debearded
- 1 teaspoon sesame oil
- 1 scallion, both white and green parts, chopped into 1-inch pieces

To make the sauce

INSTRUCTIONS:

1. Mix the water, black bean sauce, rice vinegar, sugar, light soy sauce, and dark soy sauce in a small bowl. Mix well, then put to the side. How to make stir-fried food

2. Over medium-high heat, heat the oil in the wok until it shines.
3. Stir-fry the ginger and garlic until they smell good, which should take about 20 seconds.
4. The mussels and sauce should be put in the pot. Bring the heat down and stir.
5. Cover the pot and stir the food every minute for about five minutes.
6. Turn off the heat and stir in the sesame oil and onions when most mussel shells have opened. Discard any fresh mussels.
7. Move to a dish to serve and do so right away.

SESAME SHRIMP, SWEET PEPPER, AND CUCUMBER STIR-FRY (ZI MA HA)

This stir-fry has sweet and sour flavours and is easy and quick to make. It contains fresh cucumber and red bell pepper. Bell peppers that are red are just riper and sweeter than green bell peppers.

INGREDIENTS:

- 8 ounces large shrimp, shelled, deveined, and cut in half lengthwise
- 2 tablespoons Shaoxing cooking wine
- 2 tablespoons rice vinegar
- 1 tablespoon toasted sesame oil
- 1 (8-ounce) can pineapple chunks packed in juice; juice strained and divided

- 1 tablespoon cornstarch
- 2 tablespoons cooking oil
- 1 teaspoon chopped fresh ginger
- 2 garlic cloves, crushed and chopped
- 1 medium sweet red bell pepper, diced into ½-inch pieces
- 1 medium cucumber, skin on, diced into
- ½-inch pieces
- 4 scallions, both white and green parts, cut into ¼-inch pieces
- 1 tablespoon toasted sesame seeds
- Rice or noodles for serving

INSTRUCTIONS:

1. Mix the shrimp, wine, vinegar, sesame oil, pineapple juice, and cornstarch in a medium bowl.
2. Over medium-high heat, heat the oil in the wok until it shines.
3. Stir-fry the ginger, garlic, and shrimp for one minute until the food smells good. Be sure to save the shrimp's juice.
4. Stir-fry the pineapple pieces for one minute to combine everything.
5. Stir-fry the bell pepper and onion for one minute to mix everything.
6. Stir-fry for a minute after adding half of the pineapple's smooth juice to make a light glaze. To make more glaze, add more liquid.
7. Add the green onions and sesame seeds and stir them in. Serve over noodles or rice.

SMOKED AND STEAMED EARL GREY TEA MUSSELS AND OYSTER SAUCE

There are a lot of live mussels from farms in grocery shops and fish markets. Mixing Earl Grey tea, rice, sugar, oyster sauce, and mussel soup is different and tastes good.

INGREDIENTS:

- 2 pounds of fresh mussels, washed and sorted
- ¼ cup uncooked long-grain white Rice
- ¼ cup loose Earl Grey tea
- 2 tablespoons chopped fresh ginger
- 4 garlic cloves, crushed and chopped
- 2 tablespoons brown sugar
- 2 tablespoons all-purpose flour
- ¼ cup water
- ½ cup oyster sauce
- Put the mussels in a 9-inch pie pan.

INSTRUCTIONS:

1. Mix the rice, tea leaves, ginger, garlic, brown sugar, and flour on a square piece of aluminium foil, and then roll up the sides to make a shallow, 12-inch-deep saucer. It should have an open top. Put the paper plate in the wok's bottom.
2. Put a rack in the wok and a shelf on top of the pie pan. Use a dome-shaped lid to cover.
3. If you're cooking inside, open any windows near the stove and turn up the speed of your vent fan. If you can't get the air out of the room, do the following steps outside.
4. Make it hotter. As the mix heats up, smoke will come out of it. At first, it will be white, then it will be a light yellow

colour, and then it will be a darker yellow colour. Turn down the heat when it turns dark yellow, which will take about 5 minutes.

5. Once the smoke goes dark yellow, wait two minutes and pour the 1/4 cup of water into the wok between the lid and the edge without taking the lid off. Keep your distance from the steam.

6. The mussels should cook for 5 minutes before you take the lid off. If the shell has opened, the mussels are dead. Mix 14 cups of the mussel broth from the bottom of the pie pan with the oyster sauce to make a dip.

VEGETARIAN MAINS

STEAMED TEMPEH WITH CHINESE BROCCOLI IN HOISIN SAUCE

Tempeh is a protein made from soybeans and fungi. It was made there for the first time a long time ago. Tempeh is made from soy, like tofu, but it is firmer and tastes like nuts and grains. It is very healthy and a major source of protein in Indonesia.

INGREDIENTS:

- 1 cup water
- 1 pound tempeh, cut into
- ½-inch cubes
- ¼ cup hoisin sauce
- 2 cups Gai Lan (Chinese broccoli) cut into
- 2-inch pieces
- 1 tablespoon toasted sesame oil
- Rice or noodles for serving

INSTRUCTIONS:

1. Bring the water to a boil in the wok over high heat. In the pan, put a rack.
2. Mix the tempeh and hoisin sauce in a pie pan or other flat dish. You should put the dish on the rack.
3. Let it steam for 8 minutes with the lid on.
4. Combine the tempeh and gai lan in the pan. Cover and steam for 2 more minutes or until the veggies are soft but firm.

5. Pour the sesame oil over the veggies, toss them, and serve with rice or noodles.

STIR-FRIED TEMPEH WITH GREEN BEANS, STRAW MUSHROOMS, AND MISO

This recipe is easy to make and doesn't take long. It has a lot of mushrooms and beans. Mushrooms are a fungus, and green beans are a kind of a plant called a "legume." Miso and tempeh are made with both. All of them are healthy and full of umami, which tastes good.

INGREDIENTS:

- 2 tablespoons cooking oil
- 1 tablespoon chopped fresh ginger
- 3 garlic cloves, crushed and chopped
- 8 ounces tempeh, sliced into
- ½-inch cubes
- 2 cups green beans cut or snapped into
- 2-inch pieces
- 2 tablespoons white or yellow miso paste
- 1 tablespoon Shaoxing cooking wine
- 1 tablespoon light soy sauce
- 1 (15-ounce) can of straw mushrooms, drained and rinsed
- Rice or noodles for serving

INSTRUCTIONS:

1. Put the oil in the wok and heat it high until it shatters. Stir-fry the ginger, garlic, and tempeh for 2 minutes or until the smell is good.
2. Stir-fry the green beans for one minute or until everything is well mixed.
3. Add the miso, wine, soy sauce, and stir-fry for 1 minute or until everything is well mixed.
4. Stir-fry the mushrooms for one minute or until everything is well mixed. Serve over noodles or rice.

STEAMED TOFU, MUSHROOMS, AND BOK CHOY IN BLACK BEAN SAUCE

Tofu is practically vegan mozzarella cheese. To make soy milk, you crush and strain soybeans. When a coagulant is added, curds and whey are made. With cheesecloth, the curd is formed into blocks of tofu. Protein, calcium, iron, and other vitamins and minerals can be found in tofu. It goes great with black bean sauce and vegetables.

INGREDIENTS:
- 1 pound firm tofu, crumbled
- 8 ounces mushrooms, coarsely chopped
- 1 cup coarsely chopped bok choy
- ¼ cup black bean sauce
- 2 tablespoons toasted sesame oil
- 4 scallions, both white and green parts, cut into ¼-inch pieces
- 1 cup water
- Rice or noodles for serving

INSTRUCTIONS:

1. Mix the tofu, mushrooms, bok choy, black bean sauce, sesame oil, and scallions in a pie pan or a small plate.
2. Bring the water to a boil in the wok over high heat. Put a rack in the wok and a shelf on top of the pie pan. Ten minutes later, cover it and let it steam. Serve over noodles or rice.

STIR-FRIED TOFU, CARROTS, AND BRUSSELS SPROUTS WITH GINGER

The best kind of tofu for stir-frying is extra-firm because it keeps its shape and structure. Carrots and Brussels sprouts in this dish taste best when cooked with ginger. If you stir-fry the three ingredients over high heat, the natural sugars will brown and caramelize, giving the dish a naturally sweet taste.

INGREDIENTS:

- 1 pound extra-firm tofu, drained and cut into
- 1-inch pieces
- ¼ cup cornstarch
- 1 tablespoon Chinese five-spice powder
- 3 tablespoons cooking oil
- 1 large carrot, roll-cut into
- ½-inch chips (1 cup)
- 1 cup Brussels sprouts, trimmed and halved
- 2 tablespoons chopped fresh ginger
- 2 garlic cloves, crushed and chopped
- 2 tablespoons Shaoxing cooking wine
- 2 tablespoons light soy sauce
- 4 scallions, both white and green parts, cut into ¼-inch pieces of Rice or noodles for serving

INSTRUCTIONS:

1. Mix the tofu, cornstarch, and five-spice powder in a bag with a zipper or a container with a lid. Make sure the covering is even on the tofu by shaking it.
2. Put the oil in the wok and heat it on high until it shatters.
3. Stir-fry for 3 minutes or until the carrots, Brussels sprouts, ginger, and garlic are lightly browned.
4. Pour the wine and soy sauce into the pot and stir-fry for one minute to mix them.
5. Stir-fry the tofu for three minutes or until it turns a golden brown.
6. Stir-fry the onions for one minute to ensure they are well mixed in. Serve over noodles or rice.

STIR-FRIED TOMATO AND EGGS (JIA CHANG CAI)

Most Chinese people learned to cook tomatoes and eggs together when they were young. This dish takes them back to childhood and is still a staple in Chinese houses. You'll have to try it to find out how good it feels. It can be eaten by itself or as part of a larger meal.

INGREDIENTS:

- 4 large eggs
- 1 teaspoon Shaoxing cooking wine
- Pinch salt Pinch freshly ground black pepper
- 2 tablespoons cooking oil
- 2 medium tomatoes, cut into wedges
- ½ teaspoon sugar

- 1 scallion, both white and green parts, cut into 1-inch pieces

INSTRUCTIONS:

1. Eggs and wine are mixed in a small bowl. Add salt and pepper, then beat everything together until it's well-mixed.
2. Heat the oil in the pot over medium-high heat until it shines.
3. Pour the egg mixture into the wok and cook for about a minute before scrambling it slowly. Take the egg out of the wok just before it starts to cook all the way through.
4. Stir-fry the tomato pieces in the wok until they start to soften.
5. Back in the wok with the beaten eggs and tomato. Then put sugar on top of the stir-fry.
6. Take the food off the heat, add the onion, and stir again before serving it on a plate.

HUNAN-STYLE TOFU

In southern China, the region of Hunan is known for dishes that are just the right amount of sweet, spicy, and salty. This famous tofu dish tastes salty because of the fermented black beans and spicy because of the bean paste.

INGREDIENTS:

- 1 teaspoon cornstarch
- 1 tablespoon water
- 4 tablespoons cooking oil, divided
- Kosher salt
- 1 pound firm tofu, drained and cut into
- ½-inch-thick squares,
- 2 inches across
- 3 tablespoons fermented black beans, rinsed and smashed
- 2 tablespoons doubanjiang (Chinese chilli bean paste)
- 1-inch piece of fresh ginger, peeled and finely minced
- 3 garlic cloves, finely minced
- 1 large red bell pepper, cut into
- 1-inch pieces
- 4 scallions, both white and green parts, cut into
- 2-inch sections
- 1 tablespoon
- Shaoxing cooking wine
- 1 teaspoon sugar
- ¼ cup vegetable broth (or chicken broth for a non-vegetarian dish)

INSTRUCTIONS:

1. Mix the cornstarch and water in a small bowl and set them away.

2. Heat 2 tablespoons of oil in the wok until it shines over medium-high heat.
3. Put a pinch of salt in the pan, and then arrange the tofu slices in a single layer. Sear the tofu for 1 to 2 minutes, turning the wok so the oil gets under it as it cooks. When the first side is golden brown, carefully flip the tofu over with a wok spoon and sear the other side for a minute or two until it is golden brown. Burnt tofu should be put on a plate and set aside.
4. Turn the temperature down to medium-low. Pour the two tablespoons of oil that are left into the pot. Add the black beans, doubanjiang, ginger, and garlic when the oil starts to smoke a little. Stir-fry for 20 seconds or until the bean paste changes the colour of the fat to a deep red.
5. Combine the bell pepper, onions, wine, and sugar in a bowl. Keep cooking for another minute until almost all the wine is gone and the pepper is soft.
6. Gently fold the cooked tofu until all of the ingredients in the wok are mixed. Cook for 45 seconds or until the tofu turns red and the onions limp.
7. Pour the water over the tofu mixture and stir gently to loosen anything stuck in the wok. Quickly mix the water and cornstarch, then add them to the wok. Slowly stir the sauce and cook on low heat for two minutes or until it becomes shiny and thick. Prepare hot.

BUDDHA'S DELIGHT (LO HAN JAI) VEGAN

Many Buddhist monks are vegans and don't eat the five smelly vegetables: chives, garlic, scallions, leeks, and onions. Buddha didn't eat these smelly vegetables because they were bad for living in close quarters and made it hard to concentrate and have a good mood while meditating. This dish is good for your gut and has all your favourite veggies. This makes it a great option for vegetarians and "Meatless Mondays."

INGREDIENTS:

- A small handful (about ⅓ cup) of dried wood ear mushrooms
- 8 dried shiitake mushrooms
- 2 tablespoons light soy sauce
- 2 teaspoons sugar
- 1 teaspoon sesame oil
- 2 tablespoons cooking oil
- 2 peeled, fresh ginger slices, each about the size of a quarter Kosher salt
- 1 Delicata squash, halved, seeded, and cut into bite-size pieces
- 2 tablespoons Shaoxing cooking wine
- 1 cup sugar snap peas, strings removed
- 1 (8-ounce) can of water chestnuts, rinsed and drained
- Freshly ground black pepper

INSTRUCTIONS:

1. Put the shiitake and wood ear mushrooms in their bowls and cover them with hot water. Let them sit for about 20

minutes or until they are soft. The liquid that was in the wood ears should be thrown away. Drain the shiitake mushrooms and save 12 cups of the liquid. Mix the soy sauce, sugar, and sesame oil into the mushroom liquid until the sugar is completely melted. Set aside.

2. Over medium-high heat, heat the oil in the wok until it shines. Add some ginger pieces and a pinch of salt to flavour the oil. Stir the ginger in the oil while it sizzles for about 30 seconds.

3. Stir-fry the squash for about three minutes, tossing it with the seasoned oil until it gets a light brown colour. Stir-fry for another 30 seconds after adding the two kinds of mushrooms and the wine. Add the sugar snap peas and water chestnuts and toss them around so that the oil covers them. Add the mushroom seasoning juice you saved and cover. Keep cooking, stirring now and then, for about 5 minutes or until the veggies are just soft.

4. Take off the lid and season to taste with salt and pepper. Throw away the ginger and serve.

TEA-SMOKED TOFU WITH SWEET PEPPERS AND RED ONIONS

The sweet peppers and onions go well with the smoky tea from the Wuyi Mountains in the Chinese province of Fujian. Brown sugar makes it easier for the smoke to stick to the food and get into it. For this dish, you'll need a big piece of aluminium foil.

INGREDIENTS:

- 1 pound firm or extra-firm tofu, drained, patted dry, and cut into 1-inch pieces
- 2 tablespoons light soy sauce
- ¼ cup uncooked long-grain white Rice
- ¼ cup lapsang souchong tea leaves
- 2 tablespoons brown sugar
- 1 medium red bell pepper, cut into 1-inch pieces
- 1 medium red onion, cut into 1-inch pieces
- ¼ cup hoisin sauce
- Rice or noodles for serving

INSTRUCTIONS:

1. Mix the tofu and soy sauce in a medium bowl and toss to coat.
2. Mix the rice, tea leaves, and brown sugar on a square piece of aluminium foil, then roll up the sides to make a small saucer about 12 inches deep. The top should be open. Place the foil plate at the bottom of the pan.
3. Mix the tofu, bell pepper, and onion in a pie plate or other flat dish. Put a shelf in the pot and a rack in it. Cover with a dome-shaped lid.

4. If you're cooking inside, open any windows near the stove and turn your vent fan to its highest setting. Follow these steps outside if you can't get the air out of the room.
5. Boost the heat. As the mixture gets hotter, smoke will come out of it. At first, the smoke will be white, then it will turn light yellow, and then it will get darker yellow. This will take about 5 minutes.
6. When the smoke turns dark yellow after 4 minutes, turn down the heat for 6 minutes.
7. Extinguish the fire. Pour the hoisin sauce over the other things and mix them gently. Serve over rice or noodles.

BOK CHOY WITH CRISPY TOFU

For this quick Cantonese stir-fry, the tofu must be drained of as much water as possible to keep it crispy (see tip below). This meal is easy to make and good for you. It has a light seasoning, and bok choy is served with it.

INGREDIENTS:

- 1 pound extra-firm tofu, drained and cut into ½-inch cubes
- 3 tablespoons cornstarch
- 1 teaspoon kosher salt
- 2 tablespoons cooking oil
- 2 tablespoons chopped fresh ginger
- 3 garlic cloves, crushed and chopped
- 2 cups sliced bok choy (about 1-inch strips)
- 1 bunch (6 to 8) scallions, both white and green parts, cut into ½-pieces
- 2 tablespoons light soy sauce
- 2 tablespoons ketchup Steamed Rice for serving

INSTRUCTIONS:

1. Mix the tofu, cornstarch, and salt in a big bag with a zip-top. Shake well to mix well.
2. Heat the oil in the pot on high until it starts to sparkle.
3. Stir-fry the tofu, garlic, and ginger for about 5 minutes or until the tofu is golden brown.
4. Stir-fry the bok choy for about a minute until it turns a bright green. After adding the onions, stir-fry for 30 seconds.
5. Mix the soy sauce and ketchup with a whisk in a small bowl. Add the sauce to the pan and stir-fry for 1 minute or until the tofu and bok choy are evenly covered.
6. Add to cooked rice.

SPICY HONG SHAO TOFU

Hong Shao, also called "red cooking," is made with soy sauce, which gives the food a strong red colour. First, the tofu is fried. The meat is then braised or steamed in soy sauce with aromatics and spices until it goes red.

INGREDIENTS:

- 1 pound extra-firm tofu, drained and cut into
- 1-inch pieces
- ¼ cup cornstarch
- 1 tablespoon Chinese five-spice powder
- 2 tablespoons light soy sauce
- ¼ cup cooking oil
- 1 tablespoon chopped fresh ginger
- 3 garlic cloves, crushed and chopped
- 1 teaspoon spicy sesame oil

- 2 tablespoons Shaoxing cooking wine
- 2 tablespoons dark soy sauce
- 2 tablespoons oyster sauce
- 4 scallions, both white and green parts, cut into ¼-inch pieces of Rice or noodles for serving

INSTRUCTIONS:

1. Mix the tofu, cornstarch, five-spice powder, and light soy sauce in a plastic bowl or bag with a zip-top. Toss the tofu to properly coat it.
2. Oil should be heated on high in a wok until it shimmers.
3. Add the ginger, garlic, and tofu, and cook it for 3 to 5 minutes in a small pan, turning it into a light brown colour on all sides.
4. Turn the heat to medium and add the wine, dark soy sauce, oyster sauce, and sesame oil. Let it cook on low heat for 15 minutes until the tastes come together. Serve over noodles or rice.

FRIED TOFU WITH SCRAMBLED EGG AND SCALLIONS

This is a quick and tasty way to add healthy protein to your diet while limiting the amount of carbs you eat. You can eat it at any time of day. And you only need five things to do it.

INGREDIENTS:

- 4 large eggs, beaten
- 8 ounces silken tofu, sliced into
- 1-inch pieces
- 2 tablespoons cooking oil
- 1 tablespoon chopped fresh ginger
- 2 garlic cloves, crushed and chopped
- 4 scallions, both white and green parts, cut into ¼-inch pieces, divided
- 1 teaspoon sesame oil
- Salt Freshly ground black pepper
- 1 tablespoon toasted sesame seeds for garnishing

INSTRUCTIONS:

1. Eggs and sliced tofu should be mixed in a medium bowl.
2. Oil should be heated on high in a wok until it shimmers.
3. Stir-fry the ginger, garlic, and half of the onions for a minute or until the garlic turns a light brown.
4. Stir-fry for 1 minute after adding the egg and tofu mix.
5. Stir-fry for a minute or until the eggs and tofu are hard. Add the sesame oil and the rest of the onions. Add salt and pepper to taste. Sprinkle sesame seeds on top and serve.

MATCHA SESAME STIR-FRIED TOFU, PEPPERS, AND BABY CORN

Buddhist monks brought the green tea powder called matcha to China over 900 years ago. They took it to Japan, where most people today still use it. It can be made into tea, but it can also be used to add taste to both sweet and savoury foods.

INGREDIENTS:

- 1 pound extra-firm tofu, drained and cut into
- 1-inch pieces
- ¼ cup cornstarch
- 1 teaspoon matcha green tea powder
- 3 tablespoons cooking oil
- 1 tablespoon chopped fresh ginger
- 3 garlic cloves, crushed and chopped
- 1 (15-ounce) can of baby corn, drained and rinsed
- 1 medium red bell pepper, cut into 1-inch pieces
- 1 tablespoon light soy sauce
- 1 teaspoon sesame oil
- 4 scallions, both white and green parts, cut into ¼-inch pieces
- 1 tablespoon sesame seeds for garnishing
- Rice or noodles for serving

INSTRUCTIONS:

1. Toss the tofu, cornstarch, and matcha powder together in a bag with a zip-top.
2. You should heat cooking oil in a pan until it shimmers.
3. Stir-fry the tofu, ginger, and garlic for two minutes or until the tofu is light brown.

4. Stir-fry the baby corn and bell pepper for one minute or until the food smells great.
5. Stir-fry for 1 minute to mix in the soy sauce, sesame oil, and onions.
6. Sprinkle sesame seeds on top and serve over rice or noodles.

STEAMED SEITAN WITH MUSHROOMS AND CARROTS

Seitan is a famous meat substitute made by rinsing wheat to eliminate the starch. As a substitute for meat, you can find it in the meat section of most grocery stores, natural food stores, and Asian markets. Seitan can be made at home, but it might take a lot of work based on the type of wheat used.

INGREDIENTS:
- 1 pound seitan, cut into ½-inch pieces
- 1 (15-ounce) can of straw mushrooms, drained and rinsed
- 1 medium carrot, julienned into matchstick-sized pieces
- ¼ cup hoisin sauce
- 1 teaspoon toasted sesame oil
- 4 scallions, both white and green parts, cut into
- ¼-inch pieces of Rice or noodles for serving

INSTRUCTIONS:
1. Mix the seitan, mushrooms, carrots, hoisin sauce, sesame oil, and scallions in a pie plate or other small dish.

2. Over high heat, bring an inch of water to a boil in the wok. Put a rack in the pan and a shelf above the pie plate. Cover it and steam it for 10 minutes.
3. Serve over rice or noodles.

STIR-FRIED SEITAN, ONIONS, AND CUCUMBERS

The sauce's sweet and salty tastes go straight into the seitan. If you want to make this meal with meat, use regular oyster sauce.

INGREDIENTS:
- 8 ounces seitan, cut into ½-inch pieces
- 2 tablespoons Shaoxing cooking wine
- 1 tablespoon light soy sauce
- 1 teaspoon toasted sesame oil
- 1 teaspoon cornstarch
- 2 tablespoons cooking oil
- 1 tablespoon chopped fresh ginger
- 2 garlic cloves, crushed and chopped
- 1 medium red onion, cut into 1-inch pieces
- 1 medium cucumber, cut into 1-inch pieces
- ¼ cup vegetarian oyster sauce or hoisin sauce
- 4 scallions, both white and green parts, cut into ¼-inch pieces
- Rice or noodles for serving

INSTRUCTIONS:
1. Mix the wine, soy sauce, sesame oil, and cornstarch with the seitan in a medium bowl.
2. You should heat cooking oil in a pan until it shimmers.

3. Stir-fry the seitan, ginger, and garlic for 2 minutes or until the meal smells great.
4. Stir-fry the onion for one minute or until it starts to get soft.
5. Stir-fry the cucumber for 1 minute or until all of the ingredients are well mixed.
6. After adding the oyster sauce and onions, stir-fry for 1 minute. Serve over rice or noodles.

SICHUAN FIVE-SPICE CRUMBLED TOFU AND VEGETABLES

The name of this dish tells you it is hot. The potatoes make this dish less spicy and make it a one-pot meal with protein, vegetables, and carbs.

INGREDIENTS:

- 1 pound extra-firm tofu, drained and crumbled
- 1 tablespoon Shaoxing cooking wine
- 1 tablespoon cornstarch
- 1 tablespoon Chinese five-spice powder
- 1 teaspoon red pepper flakes
- 1 teaspoon spicy sesame oil
- ¼ teaspoon crushed Sichuan peppercorns
- 3 tablespoons cooking oil
- 1 tablespoon fresh ginger, crushed and chopped
- 4 garlic cloves, crushed and chopped
- 1 cup Brussels sprouts, trimmed and halved
- 1 medium carrot, julienned into matchstick-sized pieces

- 1 medium potato, julienned into matchstick-sized pieces
- 2 tablespoons hoisin sauce

INSTRUCTIONS:

1. Mix the tofu, wine, cornstarch, five-spice powder, red pepper flakes, sesame oil, and Sichuan peppercorns in a bowl or a bag with a zip-top.
2. You should heat cooking oil in a pan until it shimmers.
3. Stir-fry the tofu, ginger, and garlic for two minutes or until the tofu is light brown.
4. Stir-fry the Brussels sprouts for 2 minutes or until they turn a bright green colour.
5. Stir-fry the onion and potato for 2 minutes or until they are soft.
6. Pour the hoisin sauce over the meat, mix it up, and serve.

STEAMED EGG WITH TOFU, PEPPERS, AND SCALLIONS

Eggs and soft tofu are used to make this steamed omelette. This dish is light and good for you. It has taste and colour from the chopped sweet peppers and scallions.

INGREDIENTS:

- 3 large eggs, beaten
- ¼ cup vegetable broth
- ½ teaspoon kosher salt
- ¼ teaspoon ground white pepper
- 1 teaspoon toasted sesame oil
- 8 ounces silken tofu
- 1 medium red bell pepper, diced into
- ½-inch pieces
- 1 medium red onion, chopped into
- ½-inch pieces
- 4 scallions, both white and green parts, cut into ¼-inch pieces

INSTRUCTIONS:

1. Whisk together the eggs, broth, salt, white pepper, and sesame oil in a pie pan or small dish.
2. Mix in the tofu, bell pepper, onion, and onions.
3. Bring an inch of water to a boil in the pan over high heat. Put a rack in the wok and a shelf on top of the pie pan. Cover the mixture and let it steam for 10 minutes or until it's hard.

VEGETABLE EGG FOO YOUNG

Egg foo young is a food that Chinese Americans made. In the 1800s, it was a fast and cheap way to feed people who worked on the train or in gold mines. Egg foo young is unlike an omelette from the West because it has rice and sauce.

INGREDIENTS:

- 6 large eggs, beaten
- 1 medium red bell pepper, diced into ¼-inch pieces
- 1 medium onion, chopped into ¼-inch pieces
- 4 ounces mushrooms, cut into ¼-inch pieces
- 1 tablespoon light soy sauce
- 1 cup vegetable broth
- 1 tablespoon hoisin sauce
- 2 tablespoons Shaoxing cooking wine
- 1 tablespoon cornstarch
- 4 tablespoons sesame oil, divided
- Steamed Rice for serving

INSTRUCTIONS:

1. Put the eggs, bell pepper, onion, mushrooms, and soy sauce in a small bowl and set it away.
2. Mix the broth, hoisin sauce, wine, and cornstarch in the wok until the mixture starts to bubble. After about 2 minutes, when the sauce has thickened, pour it into a gravy boat or a small dish.
3. Heat 1 tablespoon of sesame oil until it shimmers in the pot.
4. Add a quarter of the egg and veggie mixture to the wok and let it cook for another two or three minutes, or until the bottom is light brown, before flipping it over to brown the other side.

5. To make four plates, take the omelette off the pan and make it three more times.
6. If you have to, heat the sauce and put it on top of steamed rice.

CROSSING THE BRIDGE NOODLES (GUOGIAO MIXIAN)

Rice noodles are used to make this famous Chinese dish from the province of Yunan. The name comes from a love story about a scholar's wife who brought her husband fresh noodles daily while he was learning.

INGREDIENTS:

- 2 tablespoons cooking oil
- 1 tablespoon chopped fresh ginger
- 3 garlic cloves, crushed and chopped
- 4 ounces ground pork
- 4 ounces boneless, skinless chicken thighs, cut into ¼-inch pieces across the grain
- 4 cups broth (vegetable, chicken, beef, or seafood)
- 1 ounce sliced dried shiitake mushrooms
- 4 ounces medium shrimp, shelled, deveined, and sliced in half lengthwise
- 1 cup bok choy cut into ½-inch pieces
- 4 scallions, both white and green parts, sliced into ¼-inch pieces
- 8 ounces dried vermicelli rice noodles

INSTRUCTIONS:

1. Put the oil in the wok and heat it on high until it shatters.
2. Stir-fry the ginger, garlic, pork, and chicken for 3 minutes or until the smell is good.

3. Bring to a boil the stock and dried mushrooms.
4. Add the shrimp and cook for 1 to 2 minutes or until they turn clear and curl.
5. Add the bok choy and onions, and cook for about 1 minute or until the pork and chicken are lightly browned.
6. Turn off the heat and stir the vermicelli noodles into the broth for 2 minutes or until they are al dente.
7. Move the softened noodles to the warm bowls ("crossing the bridge"), split the other ingredients between the bowls, pour the hot broth in last, and serve right away.

MONGOLIAN BEEF AND NOODLES

This stir-fry can be made fast with thinly sliced beef and hoisin sauce. It has a little bit of heat and is sweet. Spicy sesame oil and five-spice powder add heat. You can serve this dish with rice or wheat noodles.

INGREDIENTS:

- 1 pound shaved steak, cut across the grain into 2-inch pieces
- 2 tablespoons Shaoxing cooking wine
- 1 teaspoon cornstarch
- 1 teaspoon Chinese five-spice powder
- 1 tablespoon brown sugar
- 8 ounces dried or 1 pound fresh lo mein noodles
- 1 tablespoon spicy sesame oil
- 2 tablespoons cooking oil
- 1 tablespoon chopped fresh ginger
- 3 garlic cloves, crushed and chopped
- 1 medium onion, cut into 1-inch pieces
- 1 medium red bell pepper, cut into 1-inch pieces

- 2 tablespoons hoisin sauce
- 4 scallions, both white and green parts, cut into ¼-inch pieces

INSTRUCTIONS:

1. Combine the steak, wine, cornstarch, five-spice powder, and brown sugar in a big bowl.
2. In a big pot, the noodles are cooked and then drained. Then, sesame oil is used to coat them well, and they are set away.
3. Oil should be heated on high in a wok until it shimmers.
4. Stir-fry the ginger, garlic, and onion for 1 minute or until they start to smell good.
5. Stir-fry the steak for one minute or until it is lightly browned.
6. Stir-fry the bell pepper for one minute or until it smells good but is still crisp.
7. Stir-fry the noodles, hoisin sauce, and onions together for 1 minute. Serve right away.

CUMIN LAMB NOODLES (BIANG BIANG MEIN)

This spicy dish comes from Xi'an, which is the capital of the Chinese region of Shaanxi and one end of the Silk Road. One place where the Silk Road comes to an end is Xi'an. Also, it is one of China's oldest capital towns. In this recipe, instead of the wide, hand-pulled Biang noodles, pappardelle noodles are used.

INGREDIENTS:

- 8 ounces dried or 1 pound fresh pappardelle noodles
- 1 tablespoon spicy sesame oil
- 1 pound ground lamb
- 1 tablespoon ground cumin
- 2 tablespoons Shaoxing cooking wine
- 1 teaspoon cornstarch
- 1 tablespoon red pepper flakes
- 1 tablespoon brown sugar
- 2 tablespoons cooking oil
- 1 tablespoon chopped fresh ginger
- 4 garlic cloves, crushed and chopped
- 1 medium onion, diced into ½-inch pieces
- 4 scallions, both white and green parts, cut into ¼-inch slices
- Fresh cilantro for garnishing

INSTRUCTIONS:

1. Boil the noodles in a big pot until they are "al dente" (firm to the bite). Drain the food, mix in the spicy sesame oil, and set it away.
2. Mix the meat, cumin, wine, cornstarch, red pepper flakes, and brown sugar in a small bowl. Blend well.

3. Oil should be heated on high in a wok until it shimmers.
4. Stir-fry the ginger, garlic, onion, onions, and lamb for three minutes or until the meat smells good and turns brown.
5. In a stir-fry, cook the noodles for 2 minutes. Then add the cilantro, stir, and serve.

BEEF CHOW FUN (GON CHOW NGO HO)

Thin pieces of beef cooked with rice noodles in a wok sound really fun, don't they? Fun is the Chinese word for fresh, flat rice noodles that you can buy at Asian stores. But if you can't find them where you live, don't worry. Even with the widest dried rice noodles, you can still make a meal that tastes good and fills you up.

INGREDIENTS:

- ¼ cup Shaoxing cooking wine
- ¼ cup light soy sauce
- 2 tablespoons cornstarch
- 1½ tablespoons dark soy sauce
- ½ teaspoon sugar
- Ground white pepper
- 12 ounces flank steak or sirloin tips, cut across the grain into ⅛-inch-thick slices
- 1½ pounds fresh, wide rice noodles or ¾ pound dried
- 2 tablespoons sesame oil, divided
- 3 tablespoons cooking oil, divided
- 4 peeled fresh ginger slices, each about the size of a quarter Kosher salt

- 8 scallions, both white and green parts, halved
- lengthwise and cut into 3-inch pieces
- 1 cup fresh mung bean sprouts

INSTRUCTIONS:

1. Stir the wine, light soy sauce, cornstarch, dark soy sauce, sugar, and a pinch of white pepper together in a mixing bowl. To coat the meat, stir it around. Let the sauce soak in for at least 10 minutes.

2. Bring a big pot of water to a boil, then cook the rice noodles as directed on the box. Keep 1 cup of the water that was used to cook the rice and pour out the rest. Rinse the noodles in cold water and drizzle them with 1 tablespoon of sesame oil. Set aside.

3. Heat 2 tablespoons of cooking oil in the wok over medium-high heat until it shines. To make the oil taste better, add salt and ginger. Stir the ginger in the oil while it sizzles for about 30 seconds.

4. Use tongs to put the beef in the pan, and save the marinate. Press the meat against the wok for 2 or 3 minutes until a brown ring forms. Toss and flip the beef around the wok for 1 more minute. The mixture should be put in a clean bowl and set away.

5. Using the last tablespoon of cooking oil, stir-fry the onions for 30 seconds or until they are soft. If the noodles are stuck together, add some water and scoop them up. If the noodles are sticking together, add 1 tablespoon at a time of the water you saved from cooking them.

6. Put the meat back in the wok and toss it with the noodles to combine everything. Pour in the leftover marinade and stir for 30 seconds to 1 minute until the sauce thickens and covers the noodles. They should be a dark brown colour. If the sauce is too thick, add 1 tablespoon of the

water you saved while cooking. Add the bean sprouts and toss them around for about a minute until they are warm. Take out the ginger and throw it away.

7. Place on a serving dish and drizzle with the last tablespoon of sesame oil. Prepare hot.

ANTS CLIMBING A TREE (MA YI SHANG SHU)

This famous Sichuan dish was inspired by a story about a poor widow who didn't have enough money to buy food. One day, she talked a seller into giving her just a small piece of pork and a few stick noodles. When she gave the dish to her mother-in-law, she asked, "Why are there so many ants in it?" The woman said that they were small pieces of meat because she only had a small amount of food to feed them. This made her husband's mother cry, so she joked, "Let's call this dish "Ants Climbing a Tree!"

INGREDIENTS:

- 4 ounces rice stick noodles
- 1 teaspoon sesame oil
- 2 tablespoons cooking oil, divided
- 1 teaspoon chopped fresh ginger, minced
- 1 teaspoon garlic, crushed and chopped
- 2 teaspoons doubanjiang (Chinese chilli bean paste)
- 4 ounces ground lean pork
- ¼ teaspoon freshly ground black pepper
- 1 teaspoon Shaoxing cooking wine
- 1 teaspoon light soy sauce
- 1 teaspoon dark soy sauce
- ½ teaspoon sugar

- 1 cup chicken broth, Sea salt
- 1 teaspoon finely chopped red bell pepper for garnishing
- 1 scallion, finely chopped, for garnishing

INSTRUCTIONS:

1. Soak the rice noodles in a big bowl of warm water for 15 minutes or until they are soft. Drain the noodles, and then toss them with sesame oil to keep them from sticking together. Don't drink that.
2. Oil should be heated on high in a wok until it shimmers. Stir-fry the ginger and garlic until they start to smell good, about 10 seconds. Stir-fry the doubanjiang for about a minute or until it is hot and mixed well.
3. Cook the ground pork in a stir-fry until it starts to fall apart. Add the sugar, wine, light and dark soy sauce, black pepper, and water. Slowly bring to a boil. Add the noodles and stir them every so often until most of the broth is gone. Add salt to taste.
4. Bell pepper and scallion greens go on top.

VEGETARIAN FRIED RICE (SUCAI CHOW FAN)

Using cold rice from the day before is the key to making good fried rice. This dish has a lot of tasty and healthy veggies. If you're going to use it within 24 hours, you don't need to put it in the fridge. It will last about a week if you cover it in the fridge. If you freeze it, it will stay good for about a month.

INGREDIENTS:

- 2 cups leftover cooked Rice at room temperature
- 1 tablespoon toasted sesame oil
- 1 tablespoon light soy sauce
- ½ teaspoon ground white pepper
- 2 tablespoons cooking oil
- 1 tablespoon chopped fresh ginger
- 2 garlic cloves, crushed and chopped
- 3 large eggs, beaten
- 1 medium onion, diced into
- ½-inch pieces
- 4 ounces sliced mushrooms
- 1 medium red bell pepper, diced into ½-inch pieces
- ½ cup frozen corn, thawed
- ½ cup frozen peas, thawed
- 4 scallions, both white and green parts, sliced into ¼-inch pieces

INSTRUCTIONS:

1. Mix the rice, sesame oil, soy sauce, and white pepper in a big bowl. Blend well.
2. Oil should be heated on high in a wok until it shimmers.

3. Stir-fry the ginger, garlic, and eggs for about two minutes or until the eggs are done.
4. For one minute, stir-fry the bell pepper, onion, and mushrooms to mix everything together.
5. Stir-fry the corn and peas for a minute or until the peas turn a bright green color.
6. Stir-fry the rice and onions for one minute to warm and mix them. Serve. TIP: If you want fried rice but don't make enough rice for extras, you can make more rice and spread it out in a shallow baking pan or sheet. Then put it in the freezer or refrigerator for 10 to 20 minutes.

DAN DAN NOODLES (DAN DAN MEIN)

Dan dan noodles can be made in many different ways, but this street food from Sichuan is usually made with fresh white noodles in a hot broth, topped with ground pork and peanuts. Like most Sichuan recipes, this one can be very spicy, so feel free to use less Sichuan peppercorns.

INGREDIENTS:
- 1 pound fresh Chinese egg noodles (or about 8 ounces dried noodles), cooked according to package instructions
- 1 tablespoon, plus
- 2 teaspoons cooking oil, divided
- ½-inch piece fresh ginger, julienned
- 4 garlic cloves, crushed and chopped, divided
- 8 ounces ground pork
- 4 teaspoons light soy sauce, divided

- 1 teaspoon dark soy sauce
- ½ teaspoon brown sugar
- ½ teaspoon salt
- 1 teaspoon ground Sichuan peppercorns
- ½ cup chicken broth
- 2 teaspoons rice vinegar
- Pinch salt. Pinch ground white pepper
- 1 scallion, both white and green parts, chopped, for garnishing
- ¼ cup unsalted roasted peanuts, chopped, for garnishing

INSTRUCTIONS:

1. To clean the cooked noodles, run cold water from the tap over them. Make sure most of the water is gone, and then divide the noodles equally among 4 bowls.
2. Heat 2 teaspoons of oil in the pan until it starts to sparkle over medium heat. Stir-fry the ginger and half of the garlic for about 20 seconds or until they smell good.
3. Stir-fry the ground pork for 2 minutes or until it's done. Add the brown sugar, salt, and pepper, along with 2 teaspoons of light soy sauce and 2 teaspoons of dark soy sauce. Spread an equal amount of this pork mixture over the noodles in each serving bowl.
4. Stir-fry the Sichuan peppercorns, last two garlic cloves, and last tablespoon of oil for about 20 seconds.
5. Mix the chicken stock, rice vinegar, salt, white pepper, and the other 2 teaspoons of soy sauce together. Take the pot off the heat and split the broth between the bowls of pork.
6. On top of each bowl, put peanuts and chopped onions.

CANTONESE SOY AND SESAME PANFRIED NOODLES WITH SCALLIONS AND BEAN SPROUTS

This is the easiest and quickest way to make pan-fried noodles for a quick snack or to serve with stir-fry. Don't boil the noodles for too long if you want them to keep their shape and feel.

INGREDIENTS:

- 1 pound fresh or 8 ounces dried lo mein noodles
- 1 tablespoon toasted sesame oil
- 2 tablespoons light soy sauce
- ¼ cup cooking oil
- 1 tablespoon chopped fresh ginger
- 3 garlic cloves, crushed and chopped
- 4 scallions, both white and green parts, sliced into ¼-inch pieces
- 2 cups fresh bean sprouts

INSTRUCTIONS:

1. Boil the noodles in a big pot until they are "al dente" (firm to the bite). Drain the noodles, toss them with toasted soy sauce and sesame oil, and set them aside.
2. Oil should be heated on high in a wok until it shimmers.
3. Stir-fry the ginger, garlic, and onions for 1 minute or until they start to smell good.
4. Stir-fry the noodles for 2 minutes or until they get brown and crispy.
5. Turn off the heat, add the bean sprouts, and stir until everything is well combined.
6. Serve on its own or with another stir-fry.

SAMBAL PORK NOODLES

Sambal is a sauce from Indonesia that is sweet and spicy. It is made from tomatoes. Malaysia and Singapore like it a lot, too. Explorers from Europe brought red pepper from the Americas to Asia, where it is now one of the most important flavours.

INGREDIENTS:

- 1 pound fresh or
- 8 ounces dry lo mein noodles
- 1 tablespoon spicy sesame oil
- 2 tablespoons cooking oil
- 1 tablespoon chopped fresh ginger
- 4 garlic cloves, crushed and chopped
- 1 pound ground pork
- ¼ cup sambal oelek (see Ingredient tip)
- 1 tablespoon brown sugar
- 1 tablespoon ketchup
- 2 tablespoons dark soy sauce
- 1 tablespoon rice vinegar
- Chopped basil leaves for garnishing

INSTRUCTIONS:

1. In a big pot, boil the noodles until they are "al dente." Drain the noodles, mix them with the spicy sesame oil, and set them aside.
2. Over high heat, make the oil sparkle in the wok.
3. Stir-fry the pork, ginger, and garlic for 2 minutes or until the pork starts to smell good.
4. After adding the sambal oelek, brown sugar, ketchup, soy sauce, and vinegar, stir-fry the pork for 2 minutes or until it is fully cooked.

5. Stir-fry the noodles for one minute, then put basil leaves on top and serve.

SICHUAN CHENGDU-STYLE FRIED RICE (CHENGDU CHOW FAN)

Chengdu is the capital of Sichuan and the biggest city in the province, so this fried rice will have some heat. Jin Hua ham, which can only be found in China, is the main ingredient in Chengdu fried rice. Dry-cured ham from the United States is a good alternative.

INGREDIENTS:

- 2 cups leftover cooked rice at room temperature
- 1 tablespoon spicy sesame oil
- 1 tablespoon light soy sauce
- 2 tablespoons cooking oil
- 1 tablespoon chopped fresh ginger
- 2 garlic cloves, crushed and chopped
- 8 ounces cured ham, diced into ½-inch pieces
- 3 large eggs, beaten
- 1 medium onion, diced into ½-inch pieces
- 1 medium red bell pepper, diced into
- ½-inch pieces
- 4 scallions, both white and green parts, sliced into ¼-inch pieces

INSTRUCTIONS:

1. Mix the rice, sesame oil, and soy sauce in a big bowl. Blend well.
2. Oil should be heated on high in a wok until it shimmers.

3. Stir-fry the ginger, garlic, and ham for 1 minute or until the smell is good.
4. Stir-fry the eggs for about two minutes or until they are set.
5. Stir-fry the onion and bell pepper for one minute to mix everything together.
6. For 1 minute, stir-fry the rice and onions to mix them together. Serve.

CRISPY PORK BELLY FRIED RICE (SIUUK CHOW FAN)

The other ingredients in this dish taste so good because they were stir-fried in the fat from the pork belly. You could substitute uncured, thickly cut bacon if you can't find pork belly. You could also use pork butt or pig shoulder.

INGREDIENTS:

- 2 cups leftover cooked rice at room temperature
- 1 tablespoon toasted sesame oil
- 1 tablespoon light soy sauce
- 4 ounces pork belly, cut into¼-inch pieces
- 1 tablespoon chopped fresh ginger
- 2 garlic cloves, crushed and chopped
- 1 medium carrot, roll-cut into ½-inch pieces
- 1 cup Brussels sprouts, trimmed and halved
- 3 large eggs, beaten
- 1 medium onion, diced into ½-inch pieces
- 1 medium red bell pepper, chopped into
- ½-inch pieces

- 4 scallions, both white and green parts, sliced into ¼-inch pieces

INSTRUCTIONS:

1. Mix the rice, sesame oil, and soy sauce in a bowl.
2. Stir-fry the pork belly for 3 minutes over medium-high heat until it is browned.
3. Stir-fry the ginger, garlic, carrot, and Brussels sprouts for 2 minutes or until they smell good. The colour should be bright green.
4. Stir-fry the eggs for about 2 minutes or until they are firm.
5. Stir-fry the onion and bell pepper for 1 minute to mix everything together. Stir-fry the rice and scallions for 1 minute to mix everything together. Serve.

TEA-SMOKED BEEF AND VEGETABLE FRIED RICE

This fried rice takes some planning because the extra rice is cooked with brewed lapsang souchong tea, but the flavour is worth it. The tea adds a unique smokey taste to the fried rice.

INGREDIENTS:

- 2 cups leftover lapsang souchong tea rice
- 1 tablespoon toasted sesame oil
- 1 tablespoon light soy sauce
- 2 tablespoons cooking oil
- 1 tablespoon chopped fresh ginger
- 2 garlic cloves, crushed and chopped
- 8 ounces of ground beef
- 2 tablespoons Shaoxing cooking wine

- 3 large eggs, beaten
- 1 medium onion, diced into ½-inch pieces
- 1 medium red bell pepper, diced into
- ½-inch pieces
- 4 scallions, both white and green parts, sliced into ¼-inch pieces

INSTRUCTIONS:

1. Mix the rice, sesame oil, and soy sauce in a big bowl.
2. Oil should be heated on high in a wok until it shimmers.
3. Stir-fry the ginger, garlic, ground beef, and wine for 2 minutes or until the meat is brown and smells good.
4. Stir-fry the eggs for two minutes or until they are hard.
5. Stir-fry the onion and bell pepper for one minute to mix everything together.
6. For one minute, stir-fry the rice and onions to mix everything together. Serve right away.

GUILIN RICE NOODLES (MEN)

Since more than 2,000 years ago, thin rice noodles have been made in Guilin. The most famous noodles in the area are called men. People eat them for breakfast, lunch, dinner, and smaller meals. Adding chicken and spicy sesame oil to them turns into a quick and tasty wok meal.

INGREDIENTS:

- 8 cups water
- 8 ounces mifen rice vermicelli
- 1 tablespoon spicy sesame oil
- 8 ounces boneless, skinless chicken thighs, cut across the grain into ¼-inch pieces
- 2 tablespoons Shaoxing cooking wine
- 1 teaspoon cornstarch
- 2 tablespoons Guilin-style chilli sauce (such as Lee Yum Kee brand)
- 2 tablespoons cooking oil
- 4 ounces sliced mushrooms
- 4 scallions, both white and green parts, cut into ¼-inch pieces

INSTRUCTIONS:

1. Turn off the heat when the water starts to boil. Soak the dry noodles in water for 10 minutes, then drain and toss with sesame oil. Set aside.
2. Mix the chicken, wine, cornstarch, and Guilin sauce in a big bowl. Blend well.
3. Oil should be heated on high in a wok until it shimmers.
4. Stir-fry the chicken for 2 minutes or until it is just lightly browned.

5. Stir-fry the mushrooms and onions for one minute or until they are warm.

6. Stir-fry the noodles for one minute to mix them up. Serve right away.

YANGZHOU FRIED RICE (YANGZHOU CHOW FAN)

The most popular kind of fried rice in Chinese homes and restaurants is Yangzhou fried rice. Because it's so famous, some places call it "House Fried Rice." It has shrimp, scrambled eggs, chopped ham or grilled pork, and green peas. If you want, you can also add chopped carrots.

INGREDIENTS:

- 2 tablespoons cooking oil, divided, plus more as needed
- 2 large eggs, lightly beaten
- 8 ounces shrimp, peeled and deveined
- 1 small onion, diced
- ½ cup diced ham
- ½ cup frozen peas (no need to thaw)
- 6 cups cooked white or brown rice (about 2 cups uncooked)
- 1 teaspoon salt
- 2 pinches ground white pepper
- 2 teaspoons light soy sauce
- 3 scallions, both white and green parts, finely chopped

INSTRUCTIONS:

1. Heat 1 tablespoon of oil in the wok until it sparkles over medium-high heat.
2. Put the eggs in the wok, let them cook until they are hard, and then use a wok spatula to break them up. Instead of putting the eggs in the wok, put them somewhere else.
3. If you need to, add a little more oil to the pan, add the shrimp, and stir-fry until the shrimp are done. After you take the egg out, set it away.
4. Pour the last tablespoon of oil into the pan and use the wok spatula to spread it across the bottom.
5. Stir-fry the ham and diced onion until the onion is almost clear.
6. Stir-fry the frozen peas for a short time.
7. Salt and white pepper the cooked rice, and then drizzle some soy sauce over it. Stir-frying the rice for about a minute will add flavour and heat it up.
8. Back in the wok with the shrimp and beaten eggs. Add the chopped onions and stir everything together.
9. Serve right away.

EARL GREY TEA RICE WITH CHINESE SAUSAGE AND VEGETABLES

People say that Earl Grey tea was made when the Earl of Grey in England got bergamot fruit and tea from China. The lemony taste of bergamot goes well with the sweetness of Chinese sausage, which is a bit of a surprise.

INGREDIENTS:

- For this recipe, brew
- 2 cups of Earl Grey tea and use it in place of water to cook
- 1 cup of long-grain white rice.
- 2 cups cooked
- Earl Grey tea rice
- 1 tablespoon toasted sesame oil
- 1 tablespoon light soy sauce
- 2 or 3 lap Cheong Chinese sausage links, cut diagonally into ¼-inch-thick ovals
- 1 tablespoon chopped fresh ginger
- 2 garlic cloves, crushed and chopped
- 3 large eggs, beaten
- 1 medium onion, diced into ½-inch pieces
- 4 ounces sliced mushrooms
- 1 medium red bell pepper, cut into ½-inch pieces
- ½ cup frozen corn, thawed
- ½ cup frozen peas, thawed
- 4 scallions, both white and green parts, sliced into ¼-inch pieces

INSTRUCTIONS:

1. Mix the rice, sesame oil, and soy sauce in a big bowl.
2. Mix the lap Cheong, ginger, and garlic in the wok over medium heat. Stir-fry the sausage for 2 minutes to get rid of the fat, and brown it lightly.
3. Stir-fry the eggs for two minutes or until they are hard.
4. Stir-fry for 1 minute after adding the onion, mushrooms, and bell pepper.
5. For one minute, stir-fry the rice, corn, peas, and onions to mix them all together. Serve right away.
6. TIP: If you cut lap Cheong crosswise to make ovals, you'll get more surface area than if you just cut the sausage into round coins. The link will brown faster, making the stir-fry oil taste better.

VEGETABLES

SICHUAN TWO-POTATO STIR-FRY

During the Ming and Qing dynasties (1500–1900), European explorers took hot peppers, potatoes, and sweet potatoes from the Americas to trade on the Silk Road. In this dish, you can try both kinds of potatoes.

INGREDIENTS:

- 3 tablespoons cooking oil
- 1 tablespoon chopped fresh ginger
- 4 garlic cloves, crushed and chopped
- 1 large sweet potato, julienned into matchstick pieces (2 cups)
- 1 large white potato, julienned into matchstick pieces (2 cups)
- 1 tablespoon red pepper flakes
- 1 tablespoon
- Chinese five-spice powder
- ½ teaspoon ground Sichuan peppercorns
- 1 teaspoon spicy sesame oil
- 4 scallions, both white and green parts, julienned into matchstick pieces
- Rice or noodles for serving

INSTRUCTIONS:

1. Oil should be heated on high in a wok until it shimmers.
2. Stir-fry the ginger, garlic, white potato, and sweet potato for 2 minutes or until the potatoes are lightly browned.

3. Add the red pepper flakes, five-spice powder, and stir-fry for one minute or until the food smells good.
4. Stir-fry for 1 minute after adding the Sichuan peppercorns, spicy sesame oil, and onions. Serve over noodles or rice.

STEAMED BABY BOK CHOY WITH GARLIC AND HOISIN SAUCE

Baby bok choy isn't just an early-picked bok choy. The size is about half that of regular bok choy. Its leaves and stems are more tender, which makes it great for steaming with a little stir-fried garlic and a light glaze of flavorful hoisin sauce.

INGREDIENTS:
- 8 baby bok choy heads, trimmed and cut in half lengthwise
- ¼ cup hoisin sauce
- 1 teaspoon avocado oil
- 2 cloves of garlic, chopped

INSTRUCTIONS:
1. Place the bok choy halves, cut side up, in a pie pan or small dish.
2. Hoisin sauce should be put on the bok choy.
3. Bring an inch of water to a boil in the pan over high heat. Put a rack in the pot and the pan on the frame. Cover and steam the veggies for 4 minutes or until they are soft but still crunchy.
4. Take the rack and bok choy out of the pot. Put the oil in the pan and heat it until it shines.

5. Stir-fry the garlic for a minute or until it turns golden brown.
6. Put the fried garlic on the steamed bok choy and serve as a side meal.

STEAMED CHINESE BROCCOLI WITH TAHINI

Broccoli, which looks like cabbage, is in the same family as cabbage. The leaves of Gai Lan are also called "Chinese kale" In this dish, the greens are cooked until they are soft and lightly covered with a sweet and spicy tahini sauce.

INGREDIENTS:
- 2 tablespoons tahini
- 2 tablespoons Shaoxing cooking wine
- 2 tablespoons dark soy sauce
- 1 tablespoon toasted sesame oil
- 1 pound Gai lan (Chinese broccoli), cut diagonally into
- 2-inch pieces, discarding the first inch of stems

INSTRUCTIONS:
1. Mix the wine, soy sauce, sesame oil, and tahini in a bowl.
2. Slice the gai lan and mix it with the sauce. Then put the mixture in a pie pan or a shallow dish.
3. On high heat, bring 1 inch of water to a boil in the wok. Place a rack in the wok and the pie pan on the frame.
4. Cover the gai lan and steam it for 3 or 4 minutes until it is soft and crisp.
5. Mix the steamed gai lan with the sauce to cover each piece again. Serve as a side dish on its own or on top of rice or noodles.

STIR-FRIED CHINESE CABBAGE WITH RED CHILE

This shows that simple things can also taste great. Napa cabbage is what they eat in China. It's easy to make this stir-fry. It's sweet from the cabbage and garlic and spicy from the chile.

INGREDIENTS:

- 1 tablespoon cooking oil
- 3 garlic cloves, crushed and chopped
- 1 fresh red chile, such as red serrano, thinly sliced
- 1 pound napa cabbage, cut into 2-inch pieces
- 2 tablespoons chicken broth or water Sea salt

INSTRUCTIONS:

1. Heat the oil in the pot over medium-high heat until it shines. Stir-fry the garlic and pepper until they start to smell good, about 15 seconds.
2. Stir-fry the cabbage for 3 minutes or until it just starts to turn brown. Stir-fry the cabbage for another 2 or 3 minutes after adding the water until it is soft but not soggy.
3. Once you add salt, it's ready to eat.

DRY-FRIED GREEN BEANS

Green beans are usually boring, but this dish makes them taste good because they are crunchy, spicy, and smoked. These green beans are fried twice to seal in the wetness and keep them soft and again to make the outside chewy. This is a Chinese dish that you can find in many Chinese places.

INGREDIENTS:

- 1 tablespoon light soy sauce
- 1 tablespoon minced garlic
- 1 tablespoon doubanjiang (Chinese chilli bean paste)
- 2 teaspoons sugar
- 1 teaspoon sesame oil Kosher salt
- ½ cup cooking oil
- 1 pound green beans, trimmed, cut in half, and blotted dry

INSTRUCTIONS:

1. Mix the soy sauce, garlic, doubanjiang, sugar, sesame oil, and a pinch of salt in a small bowl. Set aside.
2. Heat the cooking oil in the wok over medium-high heat until it pops and sizzles around the end of a wooden spoon or 375°F. Fry the beans in small amounts at a time. A single layer of beans should cover the oil. Turn them gently in the oil for 45 seconds to 1 minute, or until the beans look wrinkled. Then, put the beans on a paper towel-lined plate to drain.
3. Once all of the beans are done cooking, carefully pour any oil leftover into a container that can handle the heat. You can wipe out and clean the pot with two paper towels and a pair of tongs.

4. Put the wok back on high heat and add 1 tablespoon of the oil you kept from frying. Stir-fry the green beans with the chilli sauce mixture until the sauce boils and coats the green beans. Move the beans to a dish and serve them while they are still hot.

CHINESE BROCCOLI WITH OYSTER SAUCE (HO YEOW GAI LAN)

Gai Lan is broccoli's leafy green and earthy-smelling cousin. Gai Lan is worth the trip to an Asian speciality store, but broccolini, which is a cross between broccoli and gai Lan, is a great substitute if you don't have one nearby.

INGREDIENTS:
- ¼ cup oyster sauce
- 2 teaspoons light soy sauce
- 1 teaspoon sesame oil
- 2 tablespoons cooking oil
- 4 peeled fresh ginger slices, each about the size of a quarter
- 4 garlic cloves, peeled Kosher salt
- 2 bunches Gai lan (Chinese broccoli), tough ends trimmed
- 2 tablespoons water

INSTRUCTIONS:
1. Mix the oyster sauce, soy sauce, and olive oil in a small bowl.
2. Over medium-high heat, heat the oil in the wok until it shines. Add the ginger, garlic, and a little bit of salt. Let

the aromatics sizzle in the oil for about 10 seconds as you move the pan around slowly.

3. Stir and toss the gai lan until it is covered in oil and bright green. Add the water, cover, and cook the gai lan until the stalks are soft enough to cut with a knife, about 3 minutes. Take out the ginger and garlic and throw them away.

4. Mix the food with the sauce until it is hot. Put the food on a plate to eat.

HOT AND SOUR STIR-FRY VEGETABLES

Ginger, garlic, scallions, hot chilli pepper flakes, Chinese vinegar, and lemon are used to flavour this quick stir-fry of veggies.

INGREDIENTS:

- 2 tablespoons avocado oil
- 1 tablespoon ginger root, crushed and chopped
- 2 cloves garlic, crushed and chopped
- 1 medium carrot roll cut into ½-inch pieces (1 cup)
- 1 medium yellow onion diced into 1-inch pieces
- 1 tablespoon dried crushed red pepper flakes
- 1 teaspoon spicy sesame oil
- 2 cups sugar snap or snow pea pods
- 4 ounces fresh shiitake mushrooms sliced into
- ¼-inch pieces 2 tablespoons black
- Chinese rice vinegar Grated zest of 1 lemon
- 2 tablespoons fresh lemon juice (1 lemon)
- 2 tablespoons thick soy sauce
- 1 tablespoon sesame seeds

- 4 scallions sliced diagonally into ¼-inch pieces

INSTRUCTIONS:

1. Put the oil in the wok and heat it on high until it starts to shimmer.
2. Stir-fry the ginger, garlic, and carrots in the wok for 1 minute.
3. Stir the onion and red pepper flakes for 1 minute in the wok.
4. For one minute, stir-fry the pea pods, mushrooms, and hot sesame oil.
5. Add vinegar, lemon peel, lemon juice, and thick soy sauce to the wok. Stir-fry for about 30 seconds or until a light sauce forms.
6. Add sesame seeds and onions and serve over rice or noodles.

STIR-FRIED CUCUMBERS AND SPICY PEANUT SAUCE

Most of the time, cucumbers aren't thought of as cooked vegetables, but they work well in stir-fries. In a pan, cucumbers get soft and juicy. Also, their juice has a light sweetness that goes well with other tastes and mixes easily with cornstarch to make a light glaze.

INGREDIENTS:

- ¼ cup peanut butter
- 2 tablespoons light soy sauce
- 1 tablespoon sriracha sauce
- 1 tablespoon spicy sesame oil
- 1 tablespoon brown sugar

- 2 tablespoons cooking oil
- 2 European cucumbers, roll-cut into
- 1-inch pieces (no need to peel or remove seeds)
- 1 tablespoon toasted sesame seeds for garnishing

INSTRUCTIONS:

1. Mix the peanut butter, soy sauce, sriracha, sesame oil, and brown sugar until smooth.
2. Oil should be heated on high in a wok until it shimmers.
3. Stir-fry the carrots for two minutes or until they are soft.
4. Pour in the sauce and stir-fry for a minute to mix everything together.
5. Serve as a side dish with sesame seeds on top.

SIMPLE STIR-FRIED CABBAGE

The main spices in this cabbage dish are ginger, garlic, wine, and soy sauce. With these items, the sweetness of the cabbage comes out, but they don't take over.

INGREDIENTS:

- 3 tablespoons cooking oil
- 4 cups Chinese cabbage, cut into1-inch pieces
- 1 tablespoon chopped fresh ginger
- 3 garlic cloves, crushed and chopped
- 2 tablespoons Shaoxing cooking wine
- 2 tablespoons light soy sauce

INSTRUCTIONS:

1. Put the oil in the wok and heat it on high until it starts to shimmer.
2. Stir-fry the cabbage, ginger, and garlic for two minutes or until the cabbage is soft.

3. Stir-fry for 2 minutes after adding the wine and soy sauce until everything is well mixed.
4. Serve it right away as a side dish or on top of rice or noodles.

STIR-FRIED ORANGE, HONEY, AND GINGER CARROTS

When my mom made this side dish, the veggies were always gone. The honey, ginger, and sugars that had turned into caramel were on the carrots, which made them taste like candy. Stir-frying carrots is easy and quick if you cut them into pieces about the size of a chopstick.

INGREDIENTS:
- 2 tablespoons cooking oil
- 1 tablespoon chopped fresh ginger
- 2 garlic cloves, crushed and chopped
- 2 cups carrots, roll-cut into 1-inch pieces
- 2 tablespoons light soy sauce
- 1 tablespoon grated orange zest
- 2 tablespoons freshly squeezed orange juice
- 2 tablespoons honey

INSTRUCTIONS:
1. Put the oil in the wok and heat it on high until it starts to shimmer.
2. Stir-fry the ginger, garlic, and carrots for three minutes or until the carrots are brown.
3. Stir-fry for 2 minutes after adding the soy sauce, orange zest, orange juice, and honey. The carrots should get better in taste, smell, and sweetness.

4. Add something extra.

SICHUAN EGGPLANT STIR-FRY

The eggplants in China are longer and smaller than the ones in the West. Les seeds are smaller, and the skin is not as thick. This makes it less sour and makes it good for stir-frying because it will keep its shape. If you can't find a Chinese eggplant, try to find a small Japanese eggplant or an eggplant from Italy.

INGREDIENTS:

- 2 tablespoons cooking oil
- 1 tablespoon chopped fresh ginger
- 3 garlic cloves, crushed and chopped
- 2 cups Chinese eggplant, roll-cut into 1-inch pieces
- 1 tablespoon spicy sesame oil
- 1 teaspoon red pepper flakes
- 1 teaspoon Chinese five-spice powder or
- 1 whole dried red chile
- 1 teaspoon ground Sichuan peppercorns
- 1 tablespoon Shaoxing cooking wine
- 4 scallions, both white and green parts, sliced into ¼-inch pieces
- 1 tablespoon toasted sesame seeds for garnishing

INSTRUCTIONS:

1. Oil should be heated on high in a wok until it shimmers.
2. Stir-fry the eggplant, ginger, and garlic for two minutes or until the eggplant is brown.
3. Stir-fry the eggplant for 2 minutes, or until it is soft, with the hot sesame oil, red pepper flakes, and five-spice powder.

4. Stir-fry for 1 minute, or until everything is well mixed, after adding the ground Sichuan peppercorns, wine, and onions.
5. Sprinkle sesame seeds or onions on top before serving.

STIR-FRIED BROCCOLI AND STRAW MUSHROOMS IN BROWN SAUCE

You can always tell when stir-fry is done by looking at the sauce. Aromatics and spices are stir-fried in this quick and easy recipe to make a dark, rich glaze that we love to put on veggies and rice.

INGREDIENTS:
- ¼ cup water
- 3 tablespoons Shaoxing cooking wine
- 3 tablespoons light soy sauce
- 1 tablespoon brown sugar
- 1 tablespoon cornstarch
- 2 tablespoons cooking oil
- 1 tablespoon chopped fresh ginger
- 3 garlic cloves, crushed and chopped
- 2 cups broccoli florets cut into 1-inch pieces
- 1 medium onion, cut into1-inch pieces
- 1 (15-ounce) can of straw mushrooms, drained and rinsed
- 4 scallions, both white and green parts, cut into ¼-inch pieces
- Rice or noodles for serving

INSTRUCTIONS:

1. Mix the water, wine, soy sauce, brown sugar, and cornstarch in a small bowl.
2. Put the oil in the wok and heat it on high until it starts to shimmer.
3. Stir-fry the broccoli, ginger, and garlic for two minutes or until the broccoli is a bright green colour.
4. Stir-fry the onion for 1 minute.
5. Stir-fry the mushrooms for 1 minute.
6. Stir the cornstarch mixture, then slowly pour it into the pan while stirring until a light glaze forms. Add a tablespoon of water at a time to thin the glaze.
7. Add the onions and serve over rice or noodles.

ASPARAGUS WITH LAP CHEONG CHINESE SAUSAGE AND PEANUTS

The sweet and salty tastes of lap Cheong salted sausage go well with the fresh asparagus. You can find lap Cheong in Asian stores and on the Internet. Don't use the thick "Chinese sausage" that you can sometimes find in grocery shops.

INGREDIENTS:

- 1 tablespoon toasted sesame oil
- ⅓ pound lap Cheong sliced diagonally into
- ¼-inch pieces (2–3 links)
- 2 cups of asparagus ends removed and diagonally cut and trimmed into 2-inch pieces
- 2 tablespoons Shaoxing wine
- ½ cup of peanuts coarsely chopped
- 2 tablespoons oyster sauce

INSTRUCTIONS:

1. Heat the sesame oil and lap cheong over high heat for about 2 minutes until the lap cheong is lightly browned.
2. Stir-fry the asparagus for 1 minute.
3. Stir-fry for 1 minute after adding the wine.
4. Stir-fry the peanuts for 1 minute.
5. Mix in the oyster sauce before you serve it over rice or noodles.

STEAMED MUSHROOMS WITH TOFU AND OYSTER SAUCE

You need two things for this dish. Use one wok to steam soft tofu. Stir-fry oyster or shiitake mushrooms in the other pan, add some sauce and place them on top of the tofu. If you want the food to be good for vegetarians, use oyster sauce that is made from plants.

INGREDIENTS:

- 1 pound silken tofu
- 1 (15-ounce) can of straw mushrooms, drained and rinsed
- ½ cup oyster sauce
- 4 scallions, both white and green parts, cut into ¼-inch pieces
- ¼ cup sesame oil

INSTRUCTIONS:

1. Put the block of silken tofu in a pie pan or other small dish that will fit in your wok.
2. Cut the tofu into pieces with 1-inch sides and a 1/2-inch thickness. Any liquid that isn't needed should be drained. Spread the pieces carefully across the bottom of the pan. They both share some things.
3. On top of the tofu, put the mushrooms.
4. Pour the oyster sauce over the tofu, and then put the scallions on top.
5. Bring an inch of water to a boil in the pan over high heat. Put a rack and a shelf in the wok. Put a lid on it and let it steam for 5 minutes.

6. In a different wok, skillet, or sauté pan, heat the sesame oil over high heat until it shimmers, or the end of a wooden chopstick makes bubbles when dipped in it. When you pour the oil over the warmed tofu is ready to eat.

SMOKED BABY BOK CHOY

Here is a way to give soft, crisp baby bok choy a light smoke taste. This two-step method uses high heat to make smoke that smells good and then a quick burst of steam to cook the veggies quickly.

INGREDIENTS:
- ¼ cup Earl Grey tea leaves
- ¼ cup uncooked brown rice
- Grated zest of 1 orange
- 1 tablespoon brown sugar
- 1 dozen baby bok choy, cut in half lengthwise
- 2 tablespoons toasted sesame oil
- ¼ cup water

INSTRUCTIONS:
1. Mix the tea leaves, rice, orange zest, and brown sugar on a square piece of aluminium foil. Make a shallow saucer about 12 inches deep by rolling up the ends. It should have an open top. Put the paper plate in the wok's bottom.
2. If you're cooking inside, open any windows near the stove and turn up the speed of your vent fan. If you can't get the air out of the room, do the following steps outside.

3. Mix the bok choy with the sesame oil and place it on a plate or rack so that it is an inch or two above the bottom of the pan and the smoking ingredients. Use a dome-shaped lid to cover.
4. Make it hotter. As the mix heats up, smoke will come out of it. At first, the smoke will be white, then it will be light yellow, and then it will be darker yellow. When the water gets dark yellow, after about 5 minutes, pour it into the wok without lifting the lid.
5. Let the bok choy cook for 2 minutes with the lid on. Add something extra.

STEAMED STUFFED MUSHROOMS

These stuffed mushrooms might become your new favourite dish because they are filled with ground pork and shrimp. You can find the dried shiitake mushroom caps you need for the dish at Asian grocery stores or on the internet. Fresh mushrooms can be used but don't have the strong umami flavour that dried mushrooms do.

INGREDIENTS:

- 8 ounces shrimp, coarsely chopped
- 4 ounces ground pork
- 1 teaspoon fish sauce
- 1 tablespoon Shaoxing cooking wine
- 1 teaspoon brown sugar
- ¼ teaspoon ground white pepper
- 1 tablespoon cornstarch
- 1 (8-ounce) can water chestnuts, drained, rinsed, and chopped
- 4 scallions, both white and green parts, minced

- 2 dozen medium-to-large dried, whole shiitake mushrooms simmered in water for
- 10 minutes, drained and stems removed

INSTRUCTIONS:

1. Chop the shrimp, pork, fish sauce, wine, brown sugar, white pepper, cornstarch, water chestnuts, and onions in a food processor until the mixture is smooth.
2. Fill each mushroom cap that has been turned upside down with enough of the mixture to make a small hill inside each cap. Put the lids in a pie pan or other dish with a flat bottom. Bring an inch of water to a boil in the pan over high heat. Put a rack and a shelf in the wok.
3. Cover the stuffed mushrooms and steam them for 15 minutes or until the pork and shrimp are done.

STEAMED CABBAGE ROLLS

In this dish, savoy cabbage leaves are lightly steamed and then filled with ground pork, chopped shiitake mushrooms, bean sprouts, and seasonings.

INGREDIENTS:

- 8 ounces ground pork
- 4 ounces fresh shiitake mushrooms, coarsely chopped
- 2 scallions, both white and green parts, minced
- 2 tablespoons oyster sauce
- ¼ teaspoon ground white pepper
- 1 dozen medium to large savoy
- Cabbage leaves soaked in boiling water for
- 20 seconds or until they just begin to wilt
- Oyster sauce for drizzling

INSTRUCTIONS:

1. To make the filling, chop the pork, mushrooms, onions, oyster sauce, and pepper together in a food processor.
2. Put 3 tablespoons of filling down the middle of each cabbage leaf in the shape of a cigar.
3. To cover the centre, fold the top of the leaf down an inch or two.
4. To make a roll, roll up the sides of the leaf. People can sign up until the end of the stem.
5. Place the final rolls, seam side down, in a pie pan or shallow dish.
6. Bring an inch of water to a boil in the pan over high heat. Put a rack in the wok and a shelf on top of the pie pan. Ten minutes later, cover it and let it steam.
7. Put oyster sauce on it after you take it out of the steamer. Serve.

STEAMED STUFFED BITTER MELON (KU GUA)

The sweet and crunchy water chestnuts go well with the bitter and soft bitter melon. In Asian stores, you can find bitter melon. You could also use cucumber in a pinch, but it won't taste the same.

INGREDIENTS:

- 2 tablespoons salt
- 2 medium bitter melon, ends removed and seeded, cut into
- ¾-inch-thick rings
- 1 (8-ounce) can water chestnuts, drained, rinsed, and finely chopped
- 8 ounces ground pork
- 2 tablespoons hoisin sauce
- 1 tablespoon Shaoxing cooking wine
- 1 tablespoon brown sugar
- ¼ teaspoon ground white pepper
- Toasted sesame oil for drizzling

INSTRUCTIONS:

1. Salt the bitter melon rings and mix them up well in a bowl. Let it sit for 5 minutes, then wash it well with cool water.
2. You can chop the water chestnuts in a food processor but don't make a mush. In the same bowl or food processor, use your hands to mix the ground pork, hoisin sauce, wine, brown sugar, and white pepper. Mix the filling's ingredients until they stick together and can be rolled into balls.

3. Put the bitter melon rings in a pie pan or other dish with a shallow bottom. Fill each circle by pressing a ball of filling into it, and make a small hill on top of each circle.
4. Bring an inch of water to a boil in the pan over high heat. Put a rack in the wok and a shelf on top of the pie pan.
5. It needs 15 minutes of steaming with the lid on.
6. Toast sesame oil, which can be spicy or not, and sprinkle it on top.

THE END

Made in the USA
Las Vegas, NV
18 February 2024

85962187R00115